500 Social Media Marketing Tips: Essential Advice, Hints and Strategy for Business: Facebook, Twitter, Pinterest, Google+, YouTube, Instagram, LinkedIn, and More!

Spring 2014 Edition

Website: http://www.andrewmacarthy.com
Facebook: http://www.facebook.com/500socialmediatips

Table Of Contents

Why Your Business Needs Social Media Marketing!

Social media marketing is now an indispensable tool in the arsenal of brands and businesses of all kinds, with new opportunities to build relationships, engage with customers, and increase sales like never before - and the stats back it up. An August 2013 survey by PewInternet revealed that 72% of adults in North America used social networking sites, including 78% of 30-49 year-olds and 89% of 18-29 year-olds. In addition, top technology research company, Gartner Research, predicts that social commerce sales will reach $30 billion annually by 2015. And in a Social Media Examiner poll conducted in 2013, 86% of respondents said that social media marketing is important to their business. If you're not using social media at all, or your current strategy isn't working for you as well as you hoped, now is the time to make a change.

You are about to learn over 500 expert hints and tips to effectively market your business across all of the most popular social media platforms, including Facebook, Twitter, YouTube, Google+, and Pinterest, many of which you can employ to make positive impacts to your social media strategy in mere minutes! Each chapter is grouped broadly into several categories, including optimizing your profile on the social network in question, and what types of content to post in order to make the most out of what each site has to offer. While each chapter is platform-specific, I strongly encourage you to read every one (even for social networks you think you might not be interested in), as you may find that unexpected crossovers in themes and ideas prove extremely useful.

The success in social media marketing comes from building strong and long-lasting relationships with customers and professional contacts over many months and years, and relaying to them the type of content and expertise that they will want to share with their friends, family, and colleagues. This approach will help to attract and keep loyal customers and connections, and get them to sell your business for you, and not the other way around! While this approach is a world away from the way most traditional marketing works, this open, two-way communication is now what billions of consumers around the world expect from the businesses and brands to whom they invest time and money.

I hope you find these 500 Social Media Marketing Tips helpful, whether you're a complete social media novice or a savvy individual looking for some extra expert tips to drive your business onto bigger and better things.

Andrew.

P.S. For tons of real-life, media-rich case studies to help support all of the written advice to come, be sure to check out my blog, YouTube channel, and premium video courses. For more information on these and the relevant URLs, take a look at the *Free and Premium Social Media Video Tutorials* and *About the Author* chapters of this book.

Before You Begin: Key Considerations For All Social Media Marketing

Assess which social networks will work best for you
Unless you're a big firm with the resources to plow full speed ahead into every social media platform included in this book, chances are you're going to want to focus on a couple of sites instead. Indeed, depending on the type of business you run, not every social media site is going to suit your marketing, your audience and what you are trying to achieve. In order to help you decide where to begin, identify on which social networks your target audience already "hangs out." Facebook and Twitter are a pretty much a given for the majority of brands simply due to their sheer size and influence, but more "niche" communities with their own unique attributes - still with hundreds of millions of users, mind you! - like Pinterest, Instagram, or LinkedIn, might be where you find can really make an impact. You'll learn all about what each particular social network brings to the table as they are introduced.

The best advice I can give when you're starting off is to experiment with one or two social networks on which you can invest some significant time, measure progress (or lack thereof) after using the tips listed throughout this book, and then either build on your success, or steadily begin to experiment with other platforms on which you might have better luck.

Define and assess your goals
Before you jump in and get started, it is useful to define the guiding theme(s) and overall goals of your social media strategy - is it to raise awareness of your brand? Increase sales? Strengthen loyalty? To add a focus to your marketing, stick to one overarching goal at a time as you progress, (e.g. *"I want to increase traffic to our website by 15% in the next 3 months"*) and switch it up as necessary. When you're starting off, don't aim too high at the risk

of being deflated if you don't hit your projected goal; getting really adept at all this stuff (particularly if you are taking social media marketing seriously for the first time) takes a while. For example, if you're a shoe store owner and you sell 20 pairs of shoes a day, why not aim to sell 25 per day to begin with? Adding an extra 5-10 sales a day is a lot more realistic than adding 100. After the first period of time has elapsed, evaluate where you are, where you want to go and what the returns might be along the way. Use analytics programs, social insights (likes, followers, comments), and other metrics to help you track and measure your activity - you'll find lots more on these as we go along.

Reconsider return on investment (ROI) metrics

With the above tip in mind, it is worth remembering that social media marketing return on investment is not like traditional marketing - in many ways, you may not always want to focus solely on monetary return within a fixed period. Consider metrics such as brand awareness, word-of-mouth promotion, traffic driven to your website via social media, and strengthening loyalty and engagement with existing customers. These can all be just as valuable in the long run - leading to plenty of sales over a longer period of time, rather than a short-term gain that dies off quickly.

Drop old-style communication methods and get social

Successful social media strategy requires just that - a *social* strategy. Traditional marketing techniques like TV and newspaper advertising worked because the direction of communication could only go in one direction (from brand to consumer) with little chance for reply, but social media means that this is no longer the case. Now that a two-way dialogue is firmly established and brands are under the spotlight 24/7, you must resist the urge to talk *at* people, and adapt your tone of voice and communication methods to connect with them on a human level - speaking to them in a personable manner and listening with intent, rather than just hearing and doing nothing about it. This lesson applies the same whether you are a small business employing a handful of people or a multi-national company with thousands of staff.

As you will see, there are occasions where something like the old-school method of promotion is necessary, but expect to spend the majority of your time being much more selfless, and even going out of your way to make individual customers feel special as a way to generate a good feeling about your product or service that travels way beyond that one person.

Don't over-promote: build relationships and provide value
I mention this a lot in this book, but it is such an important point. The vast majority of social media users do not visit Facebook, Twitter, Pinterest, and the like to be given the hard sell by companies; they use them to interact with family and friends. If they do "like" or "follow" brands on social media, they often do so on a whim (think about the number you already "like" or "follow"), and all but the most passionate fans won't want to see every single post you publish. In fact, it is unreasonable to think that you can even make it happen without spending a lot of money. Therefore, it is your job to convince people to invite your business, amongst all the competition, into something that is a big part of their everyday lives, and continue to earn your place - don't see it as a right, see it as a privilege. You do this by building trusting and loyal relationships, by being friendly, sharing great content, helping people with customer service issues, and earning the trust of fans (with the odd promotional post in between, of course... which if the rest of your strategy is up to scratch, your audience really shouldn't mind).

With competition up and organic (non-paid) reach (the number of people who see your content) at an all-time low, it is crucial that the content you post touches people on a personal and emotional level; the type of posts that are most likely to result in someone engaging with your brand instead of skipping right on by or being turned off. Before building content, clarify your audience's needs, wants and challenges - use market research to find out what the challenges your customers face and how you can help them overcome their problems. With social media content in mind, change your mindset from 'what can we sell you?' to 'what can we do to help you?'.

One useful exercise to help you keep on track is as follows: from time to time, stop and take a look at your last 10 social media posts and ask yourself this question: *"What value am I providing and what purpose am I serving?"* If you cannot clearly define the answer to this question, you should think carefully about amending your strategy to better reach audiences who are now smarter and savvier than ever before; people who easily look past weak content or an over-the-top sales message. Just like in the real world, social media followers will resonate more with a brand that they can love and trust, much more than one whose sole purpose seems to be to encourage them to open their wallets at every opportunity. All of this good work will build a positive image around your brand and slowly convert into sales.

Humanize your brand and build credibility with storytelling
Storytelling with both text and visuals is an extremely powerful strategy on social media because it allows you to connect with your audience on a more personal level (who doesn't like a good story?), and elevates you from the status of two-dimensional company to a multi-layered brand. We've especially seen a shift towards visual content being given a greater sense of significance in the past couple of years. Sites like Facebook and Twitter have adapted to help images and videos take centre stage, the popularity of Pinterest and Instagram is testament to this, too - and you can't discount the success of video apps like Vine, as well as the

8

seemingly unstoppable growth of YouTube. As your own tale unfolds over the weeks, months, and years, storytelling is the content strategy that never runs dry and is also vital to encourage engagement, build community, and drive people to take out their wallets and buy. Pull back the curtain to regularly share the history of your company, the successes and challenges you face, and the lessons you learn along the way.

Of course, storytelling doesn't *have* to have a time span attached to it: sometimes a single, high quality image or video of a product or experience can say more about your brand than thousands of words ever could, and that positive influence can be even greater if the photo or video was submitted to you by a happy customer for you to share onwards in an impressive show of "we're doing things really well" example of social proof. Humanizing your brand through storytelling - especially images and videos - makes it easier to build an audience, shows that your customers are central to influencing everything you do, and encourages them to become emotionally invested, loyal brand ambassadors.

Provide great customer service, handle complaints in the best manner

Unlike in times gone by, social media gives your company instant and effective exposure to your customers 24 hours a day, 7 days a week. Customers also have similar access to *you*, and this is no more apparent than in what can only be described as a revolution in customer service. With the instantaneousness of a Facebook post or a tweet, people's expectations for a swift and effective response to their queries or problems is higher than ever, so try to be there for them as much as possible. Many social media experts will advise you to *always* reply within an arbitrary time limit of something like 30 minutes. If you employ a dedicated social media community manager, this may be possible, but for the vast majority of businesses, it just isn't a realistic target. I'd still recommend that you deal with customer service issues as soon as possible after they arise, but suggest that a response time of anything up to 24 hours (on weekends, too, if you can manage it) is acceptable to most people, as well as a lot more attainable for businesses.

Of course, the best way to avoid customer service issues being played out publicly on social media is to prevent them from happening. To facilitate this, give people several options for making contact - email, telephone, private message, and place them where people will see them easily, like in your main bio or about section. The simpler it is to contact you, the more likely a customer is to try that first to help resolve a problem, rather than spouting off angrily at you online. In addition, demonstrate your willingness to accept that problems do sometimes occur by using your social media profiles as a way to announce less-than-positive news about product or services issues. There will always be *some* fans who are upset when they read it, but they'd be a lot more aggrieved if they had discovered the issue on their own.

If someone does post their angry grievances in public about you on social media, two of the most important pointers to remember when approaching such a situation are as follows:

Don't ignore it
The longer you leave a customer complaint to sit and fester, the more angry said customer will be, and by refusing to reply to negative feedback, it looks to *everyone* like you are unwilling to deal with problems, and simply hoping that ignoring them will make them go away. Look to respond as quickly as possible, as most customers expect a swift response.

Don't delete it
Just as bad (if not worse) than ignoring negative feedback is to delete a post submitted on your profile. When the customer who

complained notices that their comment has been deleted, they will only be *even more* upset, and other fans who see what you have done (especially if the original criticism was screen-grabbed for evidence) will think ill of you, too.

In short, always respond to complaints on social media in a professional and courteous manner, and as soon as you possibly can. Be ready to acknowledge the customer's feedback (even if you don't think you were in the wrong, as going off on the defensive is a very bad tactic, too), and willing to admit your mistakes. We're all human - customers realize this and will respect you a whole lot more for being open and honest about any errors, than simply trying to sweep issues under the carpet.

Be consistent: use a social media content calendar
One of the stiffest tests facing brands on social media is to consistently publish high quality content for their fans. A company's social media presence that appears abandoned is the digital equivalent of turning your lights off. Because you're not updating online, people will assume that you're going out of business, even if the opposite is true. Since it's this consistency that can really help to boost levels of engagement (by enabling fans to anticipate your next post) and foster a stronger relationship with your audience (who will keep coming back for more), one of the best ways to help get it right is by compiling a social media content calendar.

An editorial calendar will allow you to plan your activity for weeks - or even months - in advance. This foresight will allow you to build seasonal themes into your updates, and prevent you from posting sub-par stuff just because you need to publish something. As well as planning for the big holidays like Thanksgiving and Christmas, you will also be able to map out a strategy for "mini holidays" like July 4th or Valentine's Day, occasions where fans are actively searching on social media for deals, discounts, advice, etc. Of course, spontaneous posting to social media still has a place, but for the foundations of your strategy, a content calendar is highly recommended.

I have created a free MS Excel social media content calendar, and it's free for readers of 500 Social Media Marketing Tips. For more information and to download it to use, visit this page: http://bit.ly/socialmediacontentcalendar

Adopt the 80/20 rule, wo
An easy way to balance out your social media output in a way that will keep you on the good side of your customers, and one a lot of brands already use, is the 80/20 rule. It states that you should post non-promotional content 80% of the time (your own valuable, helpful, or personable stuff, or related content linking to another source), and reserve the other 20% for being more overtly promotional. Even within this 20%, there is a broad spectrum of promotional posts, from subtle to overt selling, depending on how you believe your audience will react.

Re-purpose content across social media
It is worth emphasizing that something that might be distributed as one piece of content in the real world (a press release, say), can be marketed as four or five content pieces for social media: blog about it, tweet, make a video, share on Facebook, turn it into an infographic for Pinterest, etc. This is a fantastic strategy for making the most of your content creation, particularly if you are strapped for time or low on resources.

Automation doesn't have to be a dirty word
With so much work involved growing and maintaining a strong social media marketing strategy over a variety of channels, automating certain tasks with tools like Buffer or Post Planner

(including the sharing of "evergreen" blog posts, posting when you are asleep but your audience is not, or when you are on vacation but still want to pump out content) - can be beneficial. Do remember, though, that building strong personal relationships with genuine one-to-one interaction should remain at the core of your work, and you certainly can't automate that.

Social media sucks up time

Social media is now an essential marketing and PR tool, and should be taken seriously. If you ask an existing employee to take over responsibility for your social media output, do not expect them to be able to do it as well as their current job. If you're going the whole hog, expect it to take up *at least* 12-15 hours a week to plan, create, and schedule content, as well as interact with all manner of customer feedback. Consider employing somebody into the role of Social Media Manager full time. Alternatively, outsource your activity to a local specialist marketing firm, experts who can help you hit the ground running. If you do, ensure that they understand your brand, marketing goals, and speak your customer's language. Take an interest in how it does things - then maybe you can take this back in-house, six or twelve months down the line.

Draw up a social media policy

Write-up a social media policy that can be shared throughout the company. This involves guidelines for what employees can and can't say or do in relation to your business in social media spaces. If you choose one person to control your social media output, make sure they have a good understanding of your brand and the industry that surrounds it before you let them loose.

Social media marketing isn't free

Several years ago, social media marketing was seen as a golden opportunity to reach and promote to customers for free. In certain aspects, this was true. Now, however, with greater competition and

13

a more astute audience, paid promotion across is all-but essential. That's not to say you can't still achieve brilliant results without spending a penny, but even a nominal figure, spent well (such as $5 per day on highly targeted Facebook ads), can noticeably compound a brand's success.

Measuring with Google Analytics and other tools
The quickest and most cost-effective way to monitor social media conversions is to apply Google Analytics campaign tracking to the links post on social networks. Use these metrics to measure success:
- Cost per impression
- Cost per engagement
- Cost per soft lead
- Cost per hard lead
- Cost per sale.

Other useful tools include Facebook Insights (to measure the performance of your Facebook Page), Bit.ly (to measure click-through rates on specific links), CrowdBooster (to measure the performance of your Twitter account), and Social Mention (to track mentions of your business name, competitor names, etc. In essence, use analytics tools to set goals, see where your social media strategy is working best, and work out how your customers are finding you so that you can fine tune and optimize your efforts going forward. It is unlikely that you will nail your social media strategy on the first attempt, so evaluate your progress often and don't be afraid to test the water with new ideas, tweak old ones and repeat what works for you.

Slow and steady wins the race
Social media success does not happen overnight, and that is always worth remembering. Just like in real life, friendships and bonds between you and your audience can take a long time to build, and

some people just take longer to warm to you and convert into paying customers than others. As I mentioned previously, sometimes the metrics that don't pay off instantly (increasing brand awareness and customer retention, or improving customer service) are the ones that will have the greatest impact on conversions later on down the line. I have seen so many instances of businesses leaping into social media marketing with gusto, only to give up shortly afterwards because they did not have 1.3 million Facebook fans and a ton of sales after their first week. If you're not serious about working at social media for not just weeks or months, but years, you are already setting yourself up for failure.

On that note, ignore 'get followers fast' scams. It might be tempting to use services offered all over the web to rack up fans and followers quickly, but you'll only end up with hundreds of random strangers - or bot accounts - who don't care about you or your business. And anyway, likes and followers are really just a vanity metric. 50 interested, engaged, and loyal followers are insurmountably better than 5,000 who are not.

Above all, have fun building relationships
I know this has been mentioned several times, but never forget that social media is all about building relationships. The stronger someone acquaints with your brand, the more likely they'll remember you and pass the positive word on to their friends and family. Be consistent, present, real and genuine in all of your communication if you want to foster genuine interaction with customers on a slow and steady path to creating loyalty, sales and brand advocates for life.

Facebook Tips:
Marketing You'll Like and Share

Facebook is the most visited website in the world, with well over one billion users on desktop and mobile - and growing. As the king of social networks, your target audience is almost guaranteed to be there. Use these tips to build, brand and market your business on Facebook, as well as amass a following of highly engaged customers.

Facebook Business Page Setup Strategy

Create a Facebook Page, not a personal profile

When you sign up to Facebook for the first time, you are assigned a Personal Timeline by default. Personal Timelines, sometimes referred to as profiles, are for individual, non-commercial use. For your business to take advantage of everything Facebook marketing has to offer, you must create a separate Facebook Page. Facebook Pages look similar to personal Timelines, but provide unique tools for brands like analytics, custom tabs to host business-related information, and advertising tools. Pages do not require separate Facebook accounts and do not have separate login information from Timelines.

You can create a Facebook Page in one of three ways: by searching 'Create A Page' in the search bar at the top of the site, by clicking the 'Create A Page' button at the top of any existing Facebook Page, or by visiting https://www.facebook.com/pages/create.

Note: If you are currently using a personal profile for business purposes, there is a chance that Facebook will find and shut your account down without notice. To give you a chance to correct this error, Facebook provides a tool that will convert your personal

Timeline to a business Page, available at
https://www.facebook.com/pages/create.php?migrate. When you
convert your personal account to a Facebook Page, your current
profile picture will be transferred and all the profile's friends will be
switched to fans who "like" your Page. In addition, your account's
username will become the username for your Page, and the name
associated with your personal account will become your Page's
name (you may be able to change this if you wish - I explain how
in the next tip). No other content, including your wall posts,
photos, videos, etc. will be carried over to your new Page, so be
sure to download an archive of this data if you want to preserve it.

How to download your Facebook archive
1. Click the cog at the top-right of your Facebook account and
choose Settings.
2. Click the "Download a copy of your Facebook data" link, then
click Start My Archive.

If you are currently using your personal profile for a mix of things
- for its originally intended purpose (i.e. to interact with friends and
family) *but also* (and wrongly) for commercial use - the best thing to
do to avoid getting into trouble is as follows: halt all business
chatter on your personal Timeline, create a separate business Page,
then encourage your audience to de-friend your personal account
and head over to "like" your new Page where they can stay up to
date with your activity.

While building a Facebook Page is essential for businesses on
Facebook, there are also several ways to utilize an individual
Timeline - in a non-commercial way - to engage with customers on
a more personal level. This strategy best suits sole traders or
individuals that are also the "face" of a company. For now, we're
going to concentrate on Pages, but look out for Timeline-based

tips in the *Using Your Personal Facebook Profile to Boost Business* section at the end of this chapter.

Keep your Facebook Page name short; get it right the first time!

If possible, try to keep your Facebook Page name short, as this will help if you go on to create Facebook ads, where the headline space in the advert (often the name of your Page) is limited to just 25 characters.

You can only change the name of a Facebook Page manually if it has fewer than 200 likes, so make sure you are happy with yours very early on. If you are not happy with your Page name and it qualifies to be changed, follow these steps to do so:

1. From the top of your Page, click Edit Page.
2. Select Update Info.
3. Change the text in the Name field and save your edits.

Note: Changing your Page's name does not affect its username or Page address (explained below).

Grab a Vanity URL for your Facebook Page

Set up a vanity URL for your Facebook business page (available when you gain 25 likes), ideally named after your brand, e.g. www.facebook.com/yourcompanyname, where 'yourcompanyname' is your username. This will make it much easier for you to tell people how to find your Facebook Page. Think about it carefully, as you will only be able to change this URL *once* in future, otherwise you will have to delete your Page and start over - not good if you've built a big fan base!

To reach the 25-fan threshold quickly, invite your e-mail contacts and current Facebook friends - a community of people who already care about you and your brand - to visit and "Like" your Page via the "Build Audience" menu at the top of your Facebook Page.

Follow the steps below to change your Page's username:
1. From the top of your Page, click Edit Page.
2. Select Update Info.
3. Click Change username in the Username section.
4. Enter a new username and click Check Availability.
5. If the username you want is available, click Confirm to save it.

Page names and Facebook Web Addresses must accurately reflect Page content. Facebook may remove administrative rights or require you to change the Page name and Web Address for any Page that fails to meet this requirement.
Page names must:
i. not consist solely of generic terms (e.g. "beer" or "pizza");
ii. use proper, grammatically correct capitalization, and may not include all capitals, except for acronyms;
iii. not include character symbols, such as excessive punctuation and trademark designations; and
iv. not include superfluous descriptions or unnecessary qualifiers.

Fill in business info accurately and employ the 'About' section trick

Be sure to fill in as much of your business' essential information as you can when setting up your Facebook Page, including name, address, contact details and website (add multiple URLs by separating them with commas in the website box). Making an effort to populate makes your Page helpful to customers who can see all of your essential information in one place, and the keyword-rich blurb is also good for search engine optimization (SEO), as the text in your About section is indexed by Google. Restaurant owner? Make sure you mark down as many types of foods you

19

serve as possible in your Page's set up, to encourage visibility in Facebook search.

If you did not categorize your Page as a Local Business when setting it up, full website URLs (including the http:// prefix) added to the 'Short Description' section (*not* the "Website" section - that has its own dedicated space) will be viewable *and clickable* from the "About" section on the left-hand side of your Page when it goes live - otherwise, your opening hours, address, and telephone number will be displayed instead. With your main website URL catered for, use this extra space to feature links to ongoing offers, promotions, contests, etc. My own Facebook Page is not a Local Business, so the Short Description box has links to my book on Amazon and includes a call to action to encourage people to go click through and buy it.

Create an awesome cover photo and stick to the rules

Use the large Timeline cover photo on Facebook to effectively communicate your brand or message in one simple image (the ideal size is 851 × 315 pixels), and reinforce your brand identity with the smaller profile photo. Ideas for cover photos include a collage of your products, highlighting ongoing offer, or featuring a photo or testimonial submitted by one of your own fans - the latter will really "wow" your customer and hopefully they'll spread the word to their friends. Keep users engaged by periodically updating your cover photo and profile pic - once per month is a good target to aim for.

Every time a Facebook user "likes" your Page, a large part of your cover image (along with your profile photo) will show in the News Feed of that person's friends, inviting them to "Like" the Page too, so do your best to make the design as compelling and visually representative of your brand as possible.

Facebook most recently amended its rules about cover photos in July 2013. They read:

"Covers can't be deceptive, misleading or infringe on anyone else's copyright. You may not encourage people to upload your cover to their personal timelines."

Facebook has been known to remove the cover photos of Pages who don't follow along, so stick to them in order to avoid any nasty surprises.

Once upon a time, Facebook told Page owners that their cover photo could not feature text that covered more than 20% of its entire area. This restriction no longer applies, which means that you can include call to actions, contact details, and pricing and purchasing information about a product in your cover image to whatever extent you like. While this is mostly good news for marketers, I would still advise caution. Too much text can make a cover photo look spammy and unprofessional, so I would recommend at least some restraint, as the instant visual impact of a great cover photo cannot be understated.

While the 20% text rule has been removed for Page cover photos, it still applies to Facebook ads; we'll take a closer look at this later on in the chapter.

Add a call to action, offers and links in the cover design and description

When you upload a cover photo, click on it and you will be able to add a description. Here, type a short, related blurb, then add in a call to action and related links to your website, a product, an offer, a Page tab, or feature a discount code as a reward for clicking. Many Facebook Page visitors click on cover photos for a closer look, so use the description as a way to anchor the photo and encourage them to take action. To encourage more clicks on your cover photo, you can try experimenting with a "button" as part of your cover design with its own call to action, e.g. *"Get 10% off your next purchase with us - Click Here!"*

Alternatively (and to tempt the people who won't click on your Page's cover photo - call to action or not -), you might want to use it to let non-fans know what value there is to them in "liking" your Page, e.g. Free DIY tips, daily dessert recipes, regular parenting advice, etc.

Note: When you upload a fresh cover photo, the new image will appear as an update in the News Feed of your fans, *minus its description*. If the design features a call to action button to an offer contained within the description, you've essentially created a clickable banner ad for News Feed. It isn't a bad idea to have that call to action seen by everyone, but if you'd prefer to be more subtle, design the CTA to appear in the small area of your cover photo that is obscured by the profile photo (use my template detailed later to help you line it up right). Everyone will see the CTA when it appears in News Feeds, but it will be obscured by the profile photo when anybody visits Page.

Create a Facebook profile photo that is the perfect size
Facebook recommends a profile image that is at least 180×180 pixels because it will automatically be cropped around the edges to 160×160 square when displayed on your Page. Any image smaller than 160×160 will automatically be stretched to fit the space, and will look blurry. The best thing to do is to create a large square logo - something like 640×640 pixels (or as big as you want, really). It will automatically be scaled down to 160×160, look nice and crisp, and anyone who clicks on your profile photo for a closer look will see the large image in all its glory. As with the cover photo, edit the description of your profile photo to add some blurb

and a link to your website or an offer, as a way to reward those curious enough to have clicked it.

Free Facebook cover and profile photo template

The Facebook Page cover and profile images look quite different between desktop and mobile devices. To make creating your dream cover photo - optimized for desktop *and* mobile - as easy as possible, I have made a free template for use with Adobe Photoshop or GIMP. Once you have downloaded the template, follow the instructions within it to insert your design, then save the file as a .png ready for upload to Facebook. Grab your free template via the link in the *Free Social Media Templates* chapter of this book.

Create new Facebook Page custom tabs with static HTML

Custom tabs display in the "Apps" section on the left-hand side of your Facebook Page and are great little hub for things like promoting your products and services, hosting contests, or encouraging people to sign up to your e-mail list. One of the best ways to populate custom tabs is with the free Static HTML iframe application. To get started, find and install the Static HTML iframe app via the Facebook's search bar. As an example, I used the Static HTML app to build a 'Welcome' tab, which encourages users to 'like' my page for free social media video tutorial updates, and gives information about my book, with a clickable link to purchase it at Amazon. If the relatively basic coding required by the Static HTML iframe app is beyond your knowledge (and you don't have a developer to help you), check out "freemium" services like Pagemodo (http://www.pagemodo.com) and Woobox (http://www.woobox.com) that, through a simple step-by-step prrocess will automatically generate custom tabs for you.

Customize tab images, name them, and re-order by importance

When you install a custom tab app, it will often have a generic tab image that will hardly encourage people to click on it. Edit your Facebook Page's custom tab images (click pencil icon over tab when all tabs are showing -> Edit Settings) with pics that are ~111 × 74 pixels in dimension, to unify and enhance branding on your Facebook Page. Edit the tab name from the same menu, with a call to action, such as 'Contact Us' or 'Special Offers'. If you have multiple custom tabs on your Page, re-order them using the "Swap Position" option so that important ones appear at the top of the list.

Add a Facebook 'Like' box and share buttons to your site
To encourage visits to your Facebook Page, grab the code for a Facebook Like box (Google 'Facebook Like Box' or visit https://developers.facebook.com/docs/reference/plugins/like-box/ to find the Facebook Developers' page) and embed it in your website's sidebar. When you set up the Like box, make sure to check the options to 'Show Faces' and 'Show Posts'. This will ensure that the Like box shows viewers the profile photos of any of their friends who already like your Page, as well as a scrollable, clickable preview of your most recent status updates.

Note: Although most Facebook Like boxes are placed in website sidebars, some have had greater success by inserting them *underneath* blog posts instead. In this position, the widget works as part of a call to action, e.g. *"Did you enjoy reading my blog post? Yes? Then, click "Like" to keep in touch on Facebook..."* Why not experiment with the position of your own Like box to see which works best for you?

In addition, display both the Facebook "Like" and "Share buttons on top of, besides, or underneath the blog posts and products on your website. Doing this encourages people to broadcast their love for your work to their friends and also lets them choose how they want to do it: "Like" posts links to Facebook with one click, while "Share" allows them to add a personalized message before posting. Grab the code for these buttons by searching the web for 'Facebook Like button' (Google 'Facebook Like Box' or by visiting the Facebook Developers' page at https://developers.facebook.com/docs/plugins/like-button/.

On a related note, for access to all kinds of official Facebook brand assets for you to use online and offline (including Facebook logos and "Find Us on Facebook" badges) simply visit https://www.facebookbrand.com/

Facebook Marketing Basics

To begin the first big chunk of marketing strategy in this book, I want to address a few basic Facebook techniques, some of which can also be applied to any social media marketing, wherever you are focusing your efforts.

Post high quality content often and consistently

First and foremost, don't launch a Facebook Page and then simply let its activity dry up! One, two or three updates per day is a good target, but at a *minimum*, you should post at least a couple of times a week so that your posts continue to appear in the News Feeds of your most engaged fans - consistency is key. Here's some perspective: When someone visits their Facebook News Feed, there are an average of 1,500 possible posts that they can be shown. Add the fact that around half of users don't check Facebook every day (and, of those that do, they only browse for around 30-60 minutes in total), the chances of all of your posts being seen *and* engaged with in amongst all of that competition, falls considerably. In fact, without paid promotion (which we will look at later), Facebook makes it impossible for all of your fans to see all of your posts. Brands must now work harder than ever to eek as much free, organic reach out of their Facebook activity as possible. Facebook still offers businesses a *ton* of potential, but it is no longer as simple as it once was.

With the above points in mind, in order to make sure that as many people as possible see the content you post, it must be top quality, i.e. the kind of entertaining, helpful, inspirational, *valuable* stuff that people will like, comment, click (if a link is included) and share. In August 2013 - in an attempt to filter News Feeds to display only "high quality" content from Pages - Facebook surveyed thousands of users on what they deemed as "high quality" content, folded the responses into a new machine learning system and integrated it all with a master algorithm. The updated algorithm considers "over a thousand different factors" — including the quality of the Page's other content and the level of completion on the profile — when determining whether a post is "high quality".

The bottom line is that the more consistently engaged a customer is with your Page posts - liking, commenting, sharing - the more likely your posts are to continue to appear in their News Feed for future engagement opportunities. Facebook's News Feed Algorithm filters content into individuals' News Feeds according to what it thinks is most relevant to them. If a fan never sees posts from you (because you are inactive), ignores your posts for a prolonged period of time because they are not engaging enough (or, worse, has used the option to hide them), they will disappear from that person's News Feed and you may find it difficult to get them back in there without paying for the privilege. Research shows that it is unlikely a customer will ever voluntarily visit your Page to catch up with your posts, so do your best to make sure this situation never arises!

Don't get hung up on Facebook reach; focus on creating loyal, passionate fans

As you now know, the impact of the News Feed Algorithm means that not all of your fans will see your posts in their News Feeds when you publish them. In fact, Facebook announced in December 2013 that it expected organic reach to continue to lessen as competition for space in the News Feed increases. Therefore, you need to think less about chasing Page "likes" and post reach - as these metrics can often be arbitrary. Instead, concentrate more on producing great content that will grow you a loyal following who love what you do (and show it via post likes, comments, sharing, and word of mouth), therein encouraging *more* people to invest in your cause. **This goes not just for Facebook, but all social media.** I'd say if you're getting anywhere between 10% - 20% reach to all of your fans without paid promotion on Facebook, you're doing extremely well.

Which types of posts get the most engagement?
One of the great debates amongst marketers on Facebook is deciding whether text, photo, video, or link-share posts are the most effective in reaching fans. The truth is that nobody can tell you for certain - Facebook is always tweaking its algorithms, forcing Pages to play catch-up - and at the end of the day, it very much depends on what your individual data reveals to you is working best. For example, back in 2012 Facebook was telling us that posts that include a photo album, picture or video generate about 180%, 120% and 100% more engagement respectively than text posts alone, but what use is that potential for engagement if you notice that *your text posts* at any given point in time happen to reach 5x the amount of people than when you use images? And in January 2014, we were told that link-share posts (those that generate an automatic image thumbnail when a news article or website address is shared within a status update) should be favored because Facebook found that *"when people see more text status updates on Facebook they write more status updates themselves."*

My advice is to resist the temptation to blindly follow trends and fads that promise to deliver high levels of engagement (even the next two listed in this book!). Instead, use them as a guide but always focus on providing awesome, valuable content first. Continue to test and tweak with a close eye on your *own* stats, and keep adapting to push on with what is working best *for you* (not everybody else) at any given time.

Re-post top notch content
As not everyone will be checking Facebook all day, every day. If you have a killer article or link to share, post it several times (under different guises) throughout the day, to catch as many eyes as possible. Be careful not to be too spammy about it, though - reserve it for really important posts. I also use this technique to re-purpose old content that still has plenty of value, particularly if I think many of my newest fans might not have seen it.

Pin important posts
Facebook will allow you to pin a single post to the top of your timeline for up to a week - use this to feature important content, and make it more visible to fans who visit your Page, who might otherwise miss it as it would be shifted down the timeline as new posts are published. After creating a post, hover over it until the pencil icon appears, click it and choose 'Pin to Top'. All new status updates will appear below the pinned post until it is unpinned, whereupon it will fall into its original chronological position. Posts to consider pinning include special announcements, contents, promotions, etc.

Boost interaction with Facebook-embedded posts
In August 2013, Facebook rolled out the ability to embed personal profile or Page posts into an external website. Use embedded posts to lift conversations from your Facebook Page to help encourage and boost interaction with your posts. What's more, as

long as your status updates are public, *anybody* can embed them from your Facebook Page or re-embed them from a website, which - if your status is really shareable (with a compelling image, text, or video) - could give your Page and content a lot of exposure if it is embedded on other sites, numerous times. Embedded posts even include buttons for viewers to "Like", comment, and Share the post, *and* a button to "Like" your page.

How to embed a Facebook post
1. Hover over the post you want to embed, left-click on the arrow that appears, and choose "Embed Post".
2. Copy the code that appears and paste it as HTML on your website or blog.

Note: Just as Facebook trims long status updates in the News Feed with a "See more" link, so it does with embedded posts too. With this in mind, keep the most important information in the text of your embedded post at the start of the update.

Increase reach with re-surfaced, popular status updates
In August 2013, Facebook announced an update to its News Feed ranking algorithm that could help boost the visibility of your Page posts, which might otherwise be lost in users' News Feeds – either in the crowd of stories, or simply because the story is old and too far down the Feed to be seen when a user logs in. If a particular status update from your Page receives a lot of likes or comments, it may be chosen to reappear near the top of your fans' News Feeds to help those people who might have missed it when it was first posted. Although you should already have enough incentive to be producing top quality posts, the possibility of re-surfaced posts should bolster this mentality even further.

Guarantee reach with the "Get All Notifications" strategy

One tactic that can be used to all-but guarantee that fans see all of your Page's content is to train them to select the "Get Notifications" option, found in a drop-down menu when hovering their cursor over the "Liked" button underneath your Page's cover photo. With this selected, every time you post a new status update, the fans in question will be informed with a notification under the blue "globe" icon in the status bar of their Facebook account. This request is best communicated through a status update with a screen grab of the menu, to demonstrate the exact action that you wish them to take.

Whether or not you are comfortable with this fairly direct request at the risk of appearing pushy is up to you, and you should judge it based on the strength of the relationship you have with your audience. If you do decide to do it, I wouldn't force it upon fans very often, particularly as they are unlikely to be right on your Page when they see your instructions appear, and even more unlikely (or even unable in the case of mobile) to click through and carry it out.

Effective Facebook Page Posting Strategy

With that all out of the way, let's concentrate on some of the best practices to follow in order to give your Facebook content the best possible chance of success!

Ask questions and start discussions

A KISSmetrics study found that questions receive 100% more comments than ordinary text posts, so encourage Facebook fans to interact with you by posing questions and starting discussions. These questions can be about a product or event related to your business, or just about the wider world. The types of questions that work best include those about preference *("Do you prefer product A or product B?")*, Yes or No *(Are you a fan of X?")*, those that ask for opinions *("What's your favorite flavor of ice-cream in our range?")*, or ones that politely challenge, *("Opening our second Canadian store this month -*

guess where?"). Even the simplest question can be quite useful in achieving impressive levels of reach provided that the subject captures the attention of your audience and spurs them on to engage. Interestingly, *where* you ask the question in your status update also affects engagement rates. Posing a question at the end of your post - compared to somewhere in the middle where it can easily get ignored - can increase engagement by up to 15%, according to a study by Buddy Media.

Employ 'fill in the blanks' updates

Use 'fill in the blank' posts as a way of encouraging high levels of engagement. They're successful because fans will only have to type one or two words at the most to respond e.g. *"If you could live anywhere in the world, it would be _____."* Think about what kind of 'fill in the blank' post your Facebook fans would be interested in completing, and give it a go!

Tease content, be vague

For higher click-through rates from Facebook to external web content, be vague with your statuses on occasion. e.g. *"Summer's coming, and we have the perfect product for your vacation... [your link]."* Your fans will want to click through to see the content that you have teased...

Use hashtags to encourage engagement and conversation

In June 2013, Facebook joined sites like Twitter, Pinterest, and Google+ by rolling out the use of hashtags, which appear as clickable links in Page and personal profile updates and in posts on the news feed. Hashtags are a way of grouping similar types of content together, and can be created by typing a hash or pound symbol directly before a word while composing a status update or comment on your Page or personal profile, like this: *"What do you love about your local #walmart? Tell us using the hashtag #lovewalmart and we'll choose the best to feature on our website"* or *"It's Gap's summer sale,*

31

with up to 50% off! Come take a look... #gapsale." where "#walmart" and "#gapsale" are clickable.

Clicking on a hashtag will open up a feed where you'll see stories from the Pages and people who have posted with the same hashtag. People can use hashtags in Facebook search to discover posts related to specific topics or interests. Billions of pieces of content are shared on Facebook every day - peaking in the 8-11pm primetime slot - so hashtags provide a huge opportunity for brands and marketers to participate in conversations in a meaningful, relevant and timely way. While hashtag use hasn't blown up in the way Facebook imagined it might, used sparingly they still can be of benefit.

Several ways to use hashtags effectively on Facebook
- Use one or two strategic hashtags related to your brand or industry in your Facebook posts, particularly if they will be used for cross-platform promotion), e.g. #yourbrandname. You can also use hashtags as a way to express an emotion or sentiment relating to your post, e.g. #shoptilyoudrop, #excited, or #itstheweekend.
- Every Facebook Page has its own unique URL with a status update box at the top; the format of the URL is www.facebook.com/hashtag/yourhashtag. Drive traffic to that URL from other locations, e.g. your blog, other social networks, business cards, in-store marketing materials, etc. to encourage conversation. Use a URL shortener like bit.ly to make the link even more memorable.
- Discover new Pages and partners by searching for specific hashtags in Facebook search, and search your own hashtags to monitor what people are saying about you and your brand, then join the conversation.

Note: For more advice about the benefits of using hashtags on any social network, including the recommended formatting and amount you should use, check out the tips on hashtags in the Twitter Tips chapter of this book.

Several ways to use images for business on Facebook
Make images powerful and self-explanatory
The best images to use on Facebook are ones that catch the eye, inspire curiosity, entertain, spur emotion, or broadcast a gripping message. Research by Buffer found that self-explanatory, stand-alone images perform better than those that need explanation and clarification in the accompanying description. In essence, if your image needs a caption to make any sense at all (rather than to elaborate and provide more value), it might not be as effective.

Share a special offer, discount code, or upcoming event.
People *love* special offers, and images are a great way to highlight them in a bold and imaginative way - whether it's the launch of a season-long promotion, a one-off event, or a week where each day brings a new deal (a great way to encourage people to visit your Page multiple times). Compound an image's impact with accompanying text that includes a link for fans to access the offer/get more information, a time limit that will add a sense of urgency, and a call to action that will drive click-throughs.

Post photos of customers enjoying your products and services
There is no greater form of social proof customers showing others how much they are enjoying your product or service, and doing it with an image is extremely powerful way of converting people into customers, whether the photo is snapped by you or - even better - user-submitted. Smartphones make it extremely easy for people to snap and share experiences with your brand as they happen, so encourage your customers and fans to do just that when they are with you at your premises, out and about, or at home. Actively encourage customers to tag your Page in their photos, so that when you are notified you can easily save and share the user-

generated image on your Facebook Page (giving credit, of course, but also making the person feel special and keen to show their moment in the spotlight to their friends). Unify these types of posts with a hashtag that you can track across all platforms to hunt down more customer-generated content, and even add a subtle link to the product or service in question, if you think your audience won't mind. If you have lots of photos to show off in one go, take a look at using the Flipagram app (http://flipagram.com/) as a way to showcase them on your wall in a fun, animated, and engaging fashion.

Note: For an additional layer of persuasion, you could experiment with adding a short customer testimonial in the form of text on top of an image of happy customer, both to spread cheer about your brand and help convert others into willing buyers.

Show off product features
Add annotations to an image of a product or service to show off features that might not be immediately obvious, e.g. the special type of fabric used in a garment, how efficient your delivery times are, or the wondrous technology hidden inside a gadget. Again, don't forget to help drive sales with accompanying text, link, and a call to action.

Use the "Share to Unlock" strategy
As a way to drive organic engagement, design an image that tells fans that they'll gain access to a secret sale, discount code, etc. if said image receives a certain amount shares. Set the target small or big depending on your existing fan base and predicted reach, because you *do really* want to reach it and reward those who helped out.

Share inspirational quotes and nostalgic images

There are two types of image posts that often seem to perform really well on Facebook (and all visual social media for that matter) - and they are inspirational quotes or nostalgic images. Accompanied by a striking image, a powerful quote tends to stir an emotion in all of us, and they are also highly shareable - target your quotes to relate to the mindset of your customer. Nostalgic photos work similarly in the way that they strike a chord within us; subjects for these might include historic images of your target audience's city or neighborhood, or dusty old snaps that emote the heritage of your brand.

Optimize blog images to make an impact on Facebook
In September 2013, Facebook introduced a significant increase to the size that thumbnail images from linked articles appear in the News Feed. When you post a status update including a link, Facebook will automatically pull an image from the article, and as long as it is of sufficient size, that image will display at full width on your Page and in News Feeds, with the blog title and blurb below it.

In exact terms, for a linked article's image to display at full width on Facebook, the width of the image needs to be 1.91 times its height. Facebook recommends an image that is at least 1200 × 630 pixels, which, truthfully, isn't realistic for most bloggers. Instead, aim to produce blog posts that include at least one image that is 600 × 315 pixels (even if it an image that is uploaded large, but shrunk to fit your blog's formatting style), as this is the minimum size that Facebook requires for any linked article's image to display at full width in any position on all devices - desktop, mobile, or tablet. If your linked article's chosen image is below 600 × 315 pixels, Facebook will automatically shrink it much smaller.

Note: When you paste a link into the status box and the automatically-generated preview appears, two small arrows appear on top of the thumbnail image allowing you to select the most appealing photo from the article. If none of the available thumbnail images takes your fancy, click the "Upload Image" link and choose one that is saved on the hard drive of your computer. You can edit the text in the headline and description fields that are generated, too, if you wish to make them more effective. Check out some of the techniques listed in the Blogging Tips section of this book for more information.

On the rare occasion that you paste a link to share and no preview image appears at all, you may have to debug the page - essentially forcing Facebook to refresh its cache of your site. Simply visit the Facebook Debugger tool at https://developers.facebook.com/tools/debug, paste in the URL of the Page with the problem image, and click "Debug." Wipe your status box clean and try pasting the link again; the problem should now be fixed.

Alternate between YouTube and Facebook video
If you have videos to share, experiment by alternating between YouTube and Facebook Video. The former will get greater visibility in Google search, but being upload direct to the site, a Facebook video may be given more of a favorable ride in terms of reach (keep an eye on your analytics to see how things go). When you choose the latter option, make sure to name, tag people who feature in it, and select the best thumbnail available in the menu that appears after the content has uploaded. If the video is "evergreen" in nature (i.e. it'll still as relevant in the future as it is now) why post the video twice - once using a YouTube link and, at a later date, by uploading directly to Facebook?

Use breaking news as a marketing opportunity
One of the biggest mistakes that brands make on all social media is to post only about themselves, which can get very boring, very fast.

If you are able to weave the hot, newsworthy topics of the day into your content strategy, it can add a relevance and variety to your content that will endear you to fans. The cookie company Oreo is an expert at using this tactic. For example, at the end of 2013, it posted a short video clip accompanied by the text *"We're officially counting down to the last dunk of the year,"* and to celebrate the USA's Mars Rover robot successfully landing on the Red Planet, it posted a photo of an Oreo cookie with a red-cream centre imprinted with robot tracks, and paired it with the caption *"Now, to perfectly land an Oreo cookie in milk."*

Ask for Likes and Shares, use appropriate language

Ask users to 'Like' and Share your content when you post, so that it will be shared on their walls and in their News Feeds, therefore increasing exposure for your Page. Don't appear desperate by doing it too often, though, and word it in a way that endears you to your fans. Buddy Media found that action keywords like "post," "comment," "take," "submit," "like" or "tell us" are the most effective. Be direct in your request, and fans will listen and take action. Enhance the experience by creating a community that encourages your fans to discuss topics and interact with each other within the comments!

Keep your engagement timely

If someone comments on a status update you make or posts a public message on your wall, be sure to reply to it as soon as possible. Any chance to further the conversation, answer a query, or give thanks for a customer's support is all but lost if there is no reply – and it's something a lot of businesses on Facebook fail to do, to their detriment. If the opportunity is right, give the comments you reply to a 'Like' too - it all helps!

Note: If you're lucky enough to have a Facebook Page with over 10,000 fans or a personal profile with 10,000 or more followers, your comments section will be threaded to make replying to (your many) individual comments easier. The upgrade comes with a ranking system too, which takes into account positive signals (such as likes and comments), negative signals (such as not getting much engagement), and connections, meaning the display of comments is personalized for each individual user so that, for example, comments appear first from people they might know. This alone may help to drive more engagement with your content.

If you have fewer than 10,000 fans, you can turn threaded replies on manually. To turn on replies for your Page:

1. At the top of your Page, click Edit Page.
2. Go to Manage Permissions.
3. Select Turn On Replies.

Use @mentions to be personable and up engagement

When replying to individual fans, use the @username function to address each person individually. It'll add a personal touch to your service and make the customer in question feel special, especially as they'll receive a notification to let them know you replied. Type @ and begin typing the name of the person you want to reply to immediately afterwards. When their name appears, select it with a mouse click or the tap of a finger. If you want to be more informal and address a customer only by their first name, place your cursor at the end of their surname (after it appears in the comment box) and hit backspace a few times until their surname disappears. To that end, add a personal touch to any status updates or comments you make by 'signing' with your first name. This is especially useful if multiple admins are addressing fans on the same page.

Using @mentions can also be beneficial towards the number of people that see your Page's content. In February 2014, Facebook announced that when a Page tags another Page in a post, e.g.

"Thanks to @Perfect Pizza for supplying our prize giveaway this week - you guys rock!," it may - depending on the levels of engagement - show the post to some of the people who like or follow the tagged Page - Perfect Pizza, in this case. This kind of cross-promotion may drive traffic back to your Page - yet another reason to produce top quality posts that people want to engage with!

Use 'we' to be inclusive

Whenever addressing all of your fans, use the term 'We' to make them feel part of a shared community. If you reach a landmark (1,000 followers, say), a message like *"We did it - 1,000 followers! Thank you for all of your support!"* would go down really well and make your fans feel like a small yet valuable part of a bigger whole.

Utilize the Nearby tab and Reviews for Facebook Mobile

An update to the 'Nearby' tab of the Facebook mobile app in December 2012 means that users can use geo-location technology to find your local business, see which of their friends have visited, and whether they or the wider Facebook community have recommended you with star ratings and reviews (reviews can be submitted on mobile *or* on desktop). Given that there are over 800 million monthly mobile Facebook users, it is imperative that your profile information is filled out fully and accurately, as users can check in, call you, and find directions to businesses straight from the app too. The more reviews and check-ins you have, the more highly you will rank!

When a review is left for a business, a "story" is created that goes out to the News Feed of that customers' friends, along with the business' cover and profile photo and your star rating. At present, reviews are only enabled for Pages that are associated with a real-life physical location. However, it makes sense that Facebook will one day expand this feature to all Pages, including consumer goods, websites and other services, so whether you have a physical location or not, be sure that the About section in your profile - are filled out 100% if you want to appear.

Note: Facebook began to roll out the ability for Page owners to reply directly to reviews in February 2014. Use this function as an opportunity to thank people for the positive feedback or to courteously address any less-than-stellar comments.

Claim your Facebook Place to benefit from check-ins

Anybody can create a Facebook Place using their phone, so unless you claim that Place as your own, chances are it will be left floating around in the wilderness of Facebook picking up check-ins, while you lose out on all of the benefits. If you have your Facebook Page set up as a Place Page (this happens automatically when you set your category as Local Business and provide all of the relevant information pertaining to location), Facebook attempts to display your Page when someone tries to check in to your business. However, if it is not displayed then a customer may unwittingly create a Place for you by checking in with their phone. Worse, several Places may appear for your business if more than one customer creates a Page with slightly different spellings!

To make sure you get all of the credit for check-ins associated with your business, follow these steps to claim its Place.

1. Perform a search for your business on Facebook and filter by Places.
2. Click on your unclaimed Page and choose the cog icon menu.
3. Select "Is this your business?"
4. Follow the steps that appear on the screen. Add and verify information about your business, 'like' its address and website, and click Continue.
5. Facebook will ask you to claim your Page to prevent other people from becoming an admin without your permission. Choose

to verify your connection to the business by Email or by uploading Documentation:

Email: Choose this option if you have a business email address associated with your Facebook account. Email addresses from generic providers such as Yahoo! or Gmail will not be accepted. The email address should correspond to your business's name, such as: jane.doe@acmeproducts.com.

Documentation: Upload a scan or photo of an official document that shows your business's name and address, e.g. phone bill, business license, business tax file, articles of incorporation, etc.

6. Click Submit.

Encourage Facebook check-ins
Once you have a Place on Facebook that people can like and recommend, also remember to encourage check-ins - and make sure you check in every day too! Place notices in prominent areas of your establishment, such as the entrance, receipts and point of sale, to prompt customers to get out their smartphones, check-in and inform their friends of where they are, encouraging them to visit too - because when someone checks in, a map with your business name and profile photo pinned to it will appear in the News Feeds of that person's friends.

Build check-in deals
Facebook allows you to offer deals to customers who check in at a physical location - you choose what and how often these offers are and they're great for real-time deals and company promotion. Deals help generate awareness, encourage in-store traffic and build customer loyalty.

There are four types of deals you can create to reach different business objectives - Individual Deals (one-off offers), Loyalty Deals (awarded after a specified number of check-ins), Friend Deals (offers for groups of up to eight people), and Charity Deals (donation given to your charity of choice every time someone claims your deal). Facebook Deals are only available for a limited set of business types at present, and can be initiated from your Facebook page. They work in very similar ways to Foursquare deals, so rather than repeating myself, look out for lots of tips to make use of them in the Foursquare chapter later on.

To set up a check-in deal, go to Admin Panel > Edit Page > Update Info. At the bottom of the left-hand menu, there should be an option for "Deals". Click here, then click "Create a Check-in Deal for this Page."

Create Facebook Offers

Certain businesses can share discounts with their customers by posting an offer on their Facebook Page. When a fan claims an offer, they'll receive an email that they can show at your business' physical location or a code to enter online so that they can get the discount. If at least 50 people have liked your Page, you can create an offer. To create an offer from your Page:

1. Click Offer, Event + and click Offer from the top of the status update box.
2. Click More Options to add a start date, online redemption link or terms and conditions.
3. Preview your offer in the top left and make any changes, then click Post Offer.

Use offers to drum up activity and promote special deals, and encourage your fans to spread the word about your business to their friends. Don't forget to plan the number of vouchers you want to be available beforehand, and don't forget to give your customers a fair period of time in which to claim your offer after they have claimed it.

An example of an offer post might read, *"Visit Bob's Fresh Produce Market online today and get free shipping with purchases over $50!"* This post would be accompanied by an appealing image of beautiful and colorful fresh fruit and vegetables to catch people's eyes in the news feed and encourage engagement, of course. You might also want to consider Boosting the post as a paid campaign to increase its reach to as many of your fans as possible (more on this in a few tips' time).

When offering a special discount to Facebook fans, use plain old $5/$10/$15 off messages instead of 5%/10%/15% off, where they'd have a hassle to work out the amount. This way you'll encourage a higher buy rate.

Employ sneaky cross-page promotion

Engage and post comments (not new wall messages, this does not seem to work) on other Facebook Pages in your niche, posting under your Page's username. (Make sure you are posting as your page by selecting it from the drop-down menu at the top-right-hand side of Facebook.). A link to your Page will be visible with every comment you make, hopefully encouraging people to visit and check you out. Make your comments interesting, helpful, insightful, funny, witty, charming, etc, to increase the chances of a click-through!

Cross-promote with other Facebook Page managers

One of the most powerful ways to increase the number of genuinely interested eyes that come across your Facebook page is to work with other Page managers within your niche, or businesses local to your own. Get in touch to discuss ways in which you can occasionally cross-promote each other's Pages, share posts, conjure up offers and increase exposure for your businesses. For example, a kids' clothes store owner might get in touch with a local ice-cream parlor - places that share the same clientele - to work a cross-promotion arrangement on Facebook.

Ask to be a Featured "Like" by other Page owners

Communicate with other businesses to encourage them to add your Page to the Featured "Likes" section of their Page, and agree to do the same in return. This works great with complementary products and services, and helps spread the word of your business, as Featured Pages sit prominently on your Page, and display on rotation depending how many are set up. *To add a featured Like on your Page, Facebook Page:*

1. Visit and "Like" a complimentary business while using Facebook as your Page (or by clicking the cog underneath its cover photo, choosing "Like as Your Page..." and selecting your company's Page if you're browsing under a personal account).
2. Return to your Page and choose Edit Page > Update Page Info from the Admin panel.
3. Click "More..." and then Featured from the drop-down menu.
4. Here, click the Add Featured Likes Button and select the Page(s) you want to feature.

Share testimonials and high praise

If you receive a particularly positive message from a customer, highlight it on your Facebook Page so that all of your fans see it. Encourage fans to leave comments in your Recommendations box or add a "reviews" application to enable your customers to leave a rating and post to your Facebook page.

Add Timeline milestones, use as marketing opportunities

Facebook allows you to add Milestones in the history of your business (past and present) on your Page by scrolling through and marking dates on your timeline (e.g. when the business was established, your 1000th sale, etc.). These help flesh out your company history and can give customers a fascinating insight into your growth over the months and years (particularly if you were in business way before Facebook rolled around). You can even use upcoming milestones as a way to connect with customers and provide them with an incentive to remain engaged, e.g. *"Here's to each and every one of you for helping us reach 20,000 fans! Check back tomorrow at 6pm for a special promotion to say thanks!"*

As a twist on this strategy, and as a way to really make your customers feel a sense of ownership over your Page, why not highlight them and their stories as milestones on your Timeline? Ask fans to submit stories that explain how your product or service has affected their lives for the better, then add them - with images - as milestones that show just how much a part of your brand your customers are, and as encouragement for other people to invest in you just as much.

Hold a contest on Facebook
Facebook contests (promotions, sweepstakes and drawings) are a great way to increase awareness of your brand, generate buzz for a new product and encourage engagement on your Page. The goal of a Facebook contest should be to attract highly engaged fans who will stick with you after the contest ends and become regular customers. To this end, offer a prize that targets your audience's wants and needs (e.g. free coffee for a week, if you own a coffee shop; a free pampering session, if you own a spa). Facebook contests with generic prizes (Amazon gift cards, iPads, etc.) will attract low-value fans who aren't necessarily interested in you or your brand, and unlikely to convert to loyal fans and customers in the future. To further prevent unwanted entrants, make your contest last for a long time to put off those people only looking for the chance of a quick win (perhaps weeks or even months

depending on the prize), and also make the barrier to entry something that only true fans would take the time to do.

In a huge change to its previous guidelines, as of August 2013, Facebook once again allows contests to be administered *on Page Timelines*, not just through third-party apps like Woobox and Shortstack. As before, however, businesses cannot administer promotions on personal Timelines, and you *must* include a disclaimer releasing Facebook from liability. Now businesses can:

- Collect entries by having users post on the Page or comment/like a Page post (e.g. *"Like this post for a chance to win one of our new sandwich toasters - releasing March 21!"* or *"Comment with a funny caption for this photo - the one that makes us laugh the most / gets the most likes wins X prize."* or *"Post a photo in the comments of you using our product - our favorite will win X prize."* or *"Suggest a new menu item in the comments below, our favorite will go into production and the inventor will win X prize!"*
- Collect entries by having users message the Page (e.g. *"For your chance to win this fantastic sweat band, message us using the button above and tell us why you deserve to win!"*)
- Utilize 'Likes' as a voting mechanism, e.g. *"Help us choose our next smoothie flavor. Click 'like' to vote on your favorite pic and we'll choose one lucky person to win a $20 gift card with us!"*

While creating a promotion on a Page Timeline is faster, easier and cheaper (great for a spontaneous giveaway for example, but more likely to attract poor quality entrants), third-party apps - while requiring a small fee - still do have many advantages, and I would certainly recommend them over Timeline-only contests for bigger and more serious campaigns. Advantages of apps include:

- A more professional and customizable campaign, more in line with your branding strategy.

- More space and flexibility for content than a Page post alone, as they are hosted on a Page tab.
- The ability to collect data (such as e-mail addresses) in a secure and structured manner.
- Can require a Page "like" from users in order to enter - boosting "likes" with Timeline-only contests is difficult.
- Easier to select and contact the winner (at least it *was* until guys like Applum launched free tools to help you do so). Well worth using this tool whenever running an ad-hoc contest. Find it here: http://contestcapture.com/).

Note: In order to maintain the accuracy of Page content, you cannot tag or encourage people to tag themselves in content that they are not actually depicted in. For example, it is OK to ask people to submit names of a new product in exchange for a chance to win a prize, but it is *not* OK to ask people to tag themselves in pictures of a new product in exchange for a chance to win a prize.

Despite a relaxation in the rules for contests on Facebook, there are still important legal guidelines to follow, including offering terms of eligibility, and releasing Facebook of any association with your activity. I implore you to read the Promotions section of Facebook's Page Guidelines for a full rundown: https://www.facebook.com/page_guidelines.php

Thank your newest fans and have a fan of the month
Post a special 'Thank You' message about once a week to welcome new fans, even listing them by name if there aren't too many - find them via the "See Likes" link in your Page's Admin Panel. Doing so adds a personal touch to your communication, and reflects well on your image as a brand that cares about its audience.

To encourage engagement on your Page, launch a "Fan of the Month" initiative. By highlighting one of your most loyal fans in this way, you indirectly encourage other fans to engage more, so that they can win the coveted title the next month. For an added incentive, offer a little prize to the winner. There are several free "Fan of the Month" apps available via the Facebook search bar, and paid versions with additional options if you're interested in delving deeper.

Promote Events on Facebook

Click on the Events tab in the status update box to create your event, whether they will happen offline (like a store's grand opening) or online (like a live webinar or the start of a sale). Be sure to upload a photo of the event - a step that is often overlooked, and also build excitement with countdown statuses reminding people to confirm their attendance as the event gets closer. When you create an event, you can also add targeting so only the most relevant people will see your Page's event in their News Feeds. You're even able to target your event's invites based on criteria such as gender, location and age at the bottom of the Create New Event window. Events help promote your Page organically because when someone RSVPs to one, it will create a story in their friends' News Feed. Page admins can also easily repeat a Facebook event with the Create Repeat Event option in the drop-down box on your Event page. To get more fans on board, post the event well in advance and periodically remind (via Page posts) that it's all happening soon!

Use Facebook Graph Search to conduct audience research

Facebook's Graph Search (that's its official name) is an incredibly powerful tool for brands to discover more about the interests and attitudes of their fans (or potential fans) in order to cater future content and campaigns towards them. One of the simplest and most effective keyword strings that you can type into Graph Search for research purposes is *"Fans of [your Page name] that like [a competitor's Page name]."* Select a handful of the most relevant results and investigate these Pages to see what types of content they are using to encourage engagement and build relationships with their fans, and perhaps mirror this in your own strategy. The variables and filters on offer via Graph Search are many (including relationship status, gender, age, language, work, location, and even content they have commented on), so just play around and see what comes up! Here's some more ideas to get you started:

- *"Fans of [your Page name] that live in [your city] and are married."*
- *"Women aged over [number] who live in [our city] and that like [your competitor]"*
- *Favorite interest of people that like [Page name].*
- *"Places in [city] visited by fans of [Page name] who graduated in [year]."*

Turn on private messaging (PM)
Facebook Page owners have the option to allow customers to contact the page administrator directly (Edit Page > Message option). If you have the resources to cope with this, you should definitely leave this option on, so that customers can get in touch, particularly if they don't want to share their message on the public wall.

Divert disputes and consider the Blocklist
If conversations take a nasty turn - such as if an unhappy customer decides to rant on your wall in front of all of your fans, one strategy used by many companies is to offer the customer an alternative method of contact (email or telephone) to resolve the issue away from Facebook, thereby protecting your brand image in front of others. If you believe that this tactic is *more* likely to annoy your audience by shifting away the validation of their concerns and masking if the matter was ever settled, then try your best to solve the issue in public without causing too much of a fuss.

In other instances, where the messages posted on your wall are pure, unwarranted hate or baseless insults, you may choose to delete, report, or ignore them, *or* wait it out and see if genuine fans leap to your defense in a true sign of brand loyalty!

To ensure a safe haven for your fans, use Facebook's Moderation Blocklists to keep unwanted content off your wall too. You can add comma-separated keywords to the "Moderation Blocklist" via the Edit Page -> Manage Permissions menu. When users include blacklisted keywords in a post or a comment on your Page, the content will be automatically marked as spam.

Track your progress

Use Facebook Insights to track how your Facebook fan Page is performing day by day, and which types of updates are preferred by your audience. Discover when people engage most with your content and post during those hours. Use the 'Talking About' stats to gain a better idea of who is engaging and actively promoting your page, as opposed to who has just liked it and left.

Paid Advertising Strategy on Facebook

A budget for Facebook advertising is extremely important to consider as part of your marketing strategy, particularly because the competition for eyeballs on the site's content is ever-increasing, in tandem with the site intentionally decreasing organic (non-paid) reach. You wouldn't launch a real-world business and expect people to just turn up and continue to maintain their interest without promotion, and a Facebook Page is really no different. Luckily, you don't need to spend a fortune: Facebook ads can be a cheap and effective way to gain new fans, keep existing fans engaged, direct people to your website, or get them to do whatever function you please on the way to reaching your marketing goals.

The most basic Facebook advertising: boosting posts

To increase the ordinary reach of your most important posts - like special offers, big events, or a company milestone, Facebook encourages you to use its "Boost Post" tool, located via a button underneath each and every status update. Boosted posts last for three days and will increase the reach of your content beyond the people who see it organically. In basic terms, boosted posts create a set of instant Facebook ads, without any of the detailed customization options available through the main Facebook ads tool. For that reason, I only really recommend them if you are very pressed for time, as they don't provide anywhere near the value for money as if you use the main ads tool. Boosted posts do the following:

1. Promote your post within mobile and desktop News Feeds of Fans.
2. Promote your post within mobile and desktop News Feeds of Fans, their friends, and via a limited set of variants like age, gender, and location.
3. Generate a Sponsored Story ad within mobile and desktop News Feeds.

The eventual cost of a boosted post depends on the number of people you want Facebook to try to expose to that specific piece of content. Costs range from a maximum budget of just a dollar or two for a few thousand people, to hundreds of dollars if your aim is to reach many thousands of users. Once Facebook approves your boosted post in accordance with its "no more than 20% text if an image is used" guidelines (more on this topic below), which doesn't normally take very long, the promotion will begin.

The amount you are charged rises as your boosted post reaches more people, but if you don't feel like you are getting value for money, you can stop the promotion at any time. On a similar note, you can add to your initial maximum budget if the promotion is going better than expected. If your boosted post does not reach the number of people Facebook estimated it would reach, based on your budget over the three-day window, you will only be charged according to the number that it did reach.

To get the most out of boosted posts, do the following:
- Wait at least 5-6 hours before boosting a post - let its organic reach take hold and settle first.
- Once a post is boosted, it may take some time until it reaches the full breadth of your target audience. Will it still be relevant as much as a few days away from when it was first promoted?
- Spend money on posts that will drive meaningful engagement (not just empty "likes"), e.g. eyes on a new product or service, or clicks through to valuable information.
- Pin your boosted post to create additional visibility for the promotion.
- Measure the success of your boosted post through Facebook Insights and other analytics tools.

Note: If you boost posts and see they are getting a significant amount of negative attention (such as non-fans visiting your Page and complaining that you are spamming their News Feeds!), then you may want to re-consider how often you use this feature.

Checking your ad image adheres to the 20% text rule
Facebook places a "no more than 20% text allowed" rule on images used for ads - if your image exceeds these boundaries, your ad might be rejected during the review process, thus delaying the start of your campaign. If you want to check that your photos meet the text rule guidelines, there are a number of handy tools to help you do just that, including Facebook's own Text in Images compliance tool at https://www.facebook.com/ads/tools/text_overlay. Simply

upload a file and click the boxes to highlight the areas where text appears. The tool will count up the percentage and let you know if your image is Facebook-ready.

Beyond the Boost: Better Facebook Ads Strategy
Boosting posts is a quick and easy way to promote your Facebook content - and while it does have its place, it is limited in its scope as far as customization and targeting are concerned. Instead, when you want to promote a post or launch any type of advertising campaign, do so via the Facebook Ads tool at https://www.facebook.com/advertising From here, you can do a lot more with ads including:

- Choosing what the ad promotes depending on your goal (your Facebook Page, a particular post, a Facebook event, a custom tab with a newsletter sign-up form, an external website, etc.).
- Choosing where on Facebook the ad appears (e.g. desktop and mobile News Feeds, right-hand column).
- Adding a call to action button to ads to increase click-through rates.
- Choosing who the ad targets (based on location, age, gender, interests, and connections). Before targeting non-fans, I would suggest honing in on existing fans (many of whom won't have already seen your content or promotion organically, as well as your email list - both which Facebook enables you to do).
- Track conversions like registrations, checkouts, and key page views.

While I must stress that Facebook's main advertising tool will be suitable for the vast majority of people, some marketers now prefer to use a tool called Power Editor (http://www.facebook.com/powereditor) to create, manage, and track their ads on Facebook. If Boost Post is for beginners and Facebook's main ads tool is for the masses, then Power Editor is for the pros. It's the least user-friendly of the bunch, but includes experimental options that may be useful to those who like to micro-manage their ads, and perhaps who are running lots of campaigns at once.

Tips for Facebook ad creation
Whether you stick to Facebook's main ad-creation tool or bravely plump for Power Editor, the following pointers will help maximize the success of your promotional campaigns:

- Create at least four versions of each ad per campaign so you can experiment with different images (both promotional and more natural/lifestyle in focus), calls to action and copy so that you can clearly understand which ones are performing the best.
- Test the ad in a variety of placements (News Feed, mobile, and sidebar) to see how the results vary.
- Test a variety of target groups, based on criteria such as age, gender, Pages liked, interests, location, etc. If your advertising budget is small, hyper-target your audience. Better to serve ads to 10,000 people more guaranteed to be interested than a million where the majority might not be. To target specific individuals and those most likely to be interested in your offering, get savvy with advanced targeting options such as lookalike audiences, custom audiences, and website custom audiences in order to get the most bang for your buck.
- Use Facebook's conversion pixel plugin to track successful conversions (involves adding a piece of code to your website).
- Not hard and fast, but: use CPC / PPC (cost per click / pay per click) bids to drive web traffic and control your spend more strictly as you only pay when someone clicks, and use CPM (cost per 1,000 views) to increase brand awareness, and as a cheap way to just get seen.
- Regularly review the performance of your ads and tweak for optimum conversion going forward. Change one parameter at a

time, honing your creation until you find the one ad that delivers the best results.

I could write a whole other book on Facebook ads - much more than I have the space to include here, unfortunately. Until I do, a quick web search will return plenty of detailed step-by-step guides for making the most of Facebook ads, and I definitely recommend you do this before jumping in, getting bogged down and lost in the options available, and simply wasting your money! Typically, I only spend "big" on any ad campaign (whether it be a Boosted post or properly-planned ads) if I have a product or contest to launch, a coupon code or offer to give away, or if an organic (non-paid) post does surprisingly well and I think it has strong potential to go viral. The rest of the time, I rely on a small, but regular ad budget to help new fans find my Page.

Using Your Personal Facebook Profile for Business

As explained at the beginning of this chapter, using your personal Facebook Timeline specifically for commercial purposes is against the site's rules. However, there are a number of useful little strategies that you can implement via your individual profile that can help support your overall business marketing.

Add a Follow button to your personal profile

If you are the figurehead of your company and happy to share your personal profile's updates with customers as a way to help them feel more closely connected to you, but don't want them all to be added as friends, consider adding a Follow button to your profile via https://www.facebook.com/about/follow. Anyone who chooses to become a follower will see posts you mark as Public (toggle this option via the drop-down menu underneath the status update box) in their News Feeds. Use this ability to filter updates about your family to Friends, and updates pertinent to your business, or things that you're comfortable sharing with a wider audience to the public.

Note: Visit your Timeline settings (cog icon on your profile > Timeline Settings), then click on the "Followers" link in the menu. From here, you can adjust your Follower settings and also grab code that you can use to embed a "Follow" button on your website, too.

Create custom lists to target business-y posts to friends
Related to the tactic above, Facebook's custom lists feature allows you to target status updates to customized groups of people who are also connected to you as friends. Again, these shouldn't be promotional or commercial in nature, but perhaps stuff like news and events occurring within your industry that only a specific portion of your friend list would be interested in:

To create a new custom list:
1. From your home page, hover over the Friends section in the menu on the left and click "More."
2. Click Create List.
3. Write in the list's name, e.g. "Current Customers". Enter the names of the people you want to add to this list in the Members section.
4. Click Create.

By clicking on the links that now appear in the sidebar of your Facebook account, you can easily see, comment, like, and interact with activity from people in your lists. Remember to peruse you custom lists often for opportunities to more deeply connect with your peers, building relationships that will eventually pay off as part of your business strategy.

Change your personal profile 'Work' to your business page

If people search for your business on Facebook and come across your personal profile, you'll want to make it as easy as possible for them to find your business Page too. Click on the 'Update Info' button at the top of your profile and search for your Facebook Page in the 'Where have you worked?' box and choose it when it appears in the drop-down menu. If you *don't* see your Page appear when you type its name into the box, try typing its username instead, i.e. the bit that comes after the 'www.facebook.com/' of the Page's address. For example, I would type '500socialmediatips' as my Facebook URL is www.facebook.com/500socialmediatips.

When people add their work details but don't link it properly to their business Page by selecting it from the drop-down menu, an odd "Community Page" URL is created with that same name and has a suitcase icon. If this is the case with you presently, click Edit in the About section of your profile, delete the Community Page (click the X), then add in the correct Facebook Page using the process described above.

Another link on your personal Facebook profile
Put a URL to your Facebook Page under the 'Website' area of the Contact Info section of your personal Facebook profile. This is a "soft sell" of sorts, letting your friends passively know about your business page.

Use Graph Search to expand your connections
Using Facebook's Graph Search, you have the ability to expand your network and connect with people who are influencers in your field, or interested in your work. One effective technique is to search for *"Friends of friends who work for (company)"* or *"interests liked by people who like [your page]"*. In September 2013, Facebook also added the ability to find status updates, photo captions, check-ins and comments using Graph Search - and see *when* they were written. For example, you might search *"posts about Bob's Beautiful*

Burger Joint" or *"posts written at Laura's Lunch Shack last year."* Privacy restrictions do apply to these queries, however, so they'll only show if they are written by your Facebook friends or non-friends who post publically. With Graph Search, you can quickly see who you are distantly connected to via friends of friends, and then use the Private Message feature to reach out and encourage the blossoming of a closer relationship.

Use tactical photo tagging to increase exposure for your Page and business

While it is not possible to tag your fans in photos posted to your Facebook business Page, you *can* tag an individual if the person in question is a fan of your page *and* a friend connected to you via your personal profile. When you tag a friend in a photo, they receive a notification that appears in their real time updates (that can be seen by their friends), and it may also appear in their News Feed. By tagging new photos in this way on your Facebook business Page - or as a tactic to resurface older snaps - you can increase the number of people that see them, the engagement they receive, and overall exposure for your Page and business.

Twitter Tips:
Tweet Your Way to the Top

As the site itself best puts it: *"Twitter is a real-time information network that connects you to the latest stories, ideas, opinions and news about what you find interesting. Simply find the accounts you find most compelling and follow the conversations.*

At the heart of Twitter are small bursts of information called Tweets. Each Tweet is 140 characters long, but don't let the small size fool you—you can discover a lot in a little space. You can see photos, videos and conversations directly in Tweets to get the whole story at a glance, and all in one place."

Twitter is used by millions of businesses and individuals as a way to monitor conversations about their brand, interact with customers, manage customer service issues, promote offers and so much more. A 2013 study by analytics company KISSmetric even found that Twitter users were more likely to buy from brands they follow on the site by a margin of 64 percent. In this chapter, we'll explore some of the ways to make this a reality for you.

Top Twitter username

Your Twitter username is extremely important, as it will make up part of your Twitter profile URL - the address you'll put on all of your marketing material to direct people to follow you on the social network. As you will be publicizing it to the world, try to keep your username short, simple and memorable. Most companies use their brand name as their username, so that their address reads www.twitter.com/yourbusinessname. Unlike most other sites, Twitter will allow you to change your username as many times as you like via its Settings menu, but it's worth remembering that if you've publicized one username for a while, unexpectedly switching to a new one would not make good business sense.

The Name box - a tip for businesses
Although Twitter says 'Enter your real name, so that people can recognize you' when setting up your profile, this is not best practice for businesses. Here, enter your brand or business name, as it will appear right at the top of your Twitter profile in big, bold letters.

Add your website or landing page
Pretty obvious, this one. Twitter will display a clickable web address of your choosing underneath your Bio. If you don't have a website (or want to lead visitors to a different page, such as your blog or other social media profile), type that address here instead.

Write an engaging Twitter Bio, use real names
The Twitter Bio box gives you 160 characters to let you tell people who you are and what you do. Twitter's conversational nature means that it makes good business sense to include the real name of the person handling your Twitter account here, as well as the @usernames of anyone else who tweets for your business, so that customers have several branches of support if needs be. If you do have multiple tweeters on the same account, be sure to allow space to add a 'sign off' at the end of each tweet, e.g. initials like "^AM", so customers are clear who they are corresponding with. And as consumers want to know who they're interacting with, why not include a photo of the people responding to users' inquiries in your Twitter cover design too?

Tell customers when you're available to help
Lots of customers now turn to Twitter to help solve their problems with a company, and expect a prompt reply when tweeting - studies place the expected response time at around 30

minutes or less! If you intend to use Twitter as an outlet to handle customer service queries, then it is a good idea to let people know when you will be on hand to answer questions. Is it 24 hours a day, 7 days a week, between 9AM and 5PM EST Monday to Friday? Or just 'as soon as we can'? To help reassure customers that you will respond and provide clear expectations, include information about when you will respond, and how long it will take, within your Twitter Bio or as part of your profile's background design.

Upload an effective Twitter profile image
Ditch the default Twitter avatar and use a photo of yourself or brand logo. You could even combine the two, but make sure that a face is clearly visible - Twitter's one-to-one interactions mean that people will identify much more closely with a profile that displays a person's smiling face rather than the dreaded default 'egg' image or something similarly anonymous. Twitter recommends that your profile image be uploaded at 400 x 400 pixels. To edit your header image, click the "Edit profile" button on your page and then "Change your profile photo."

Create a custom Twitter header image
In April 2014, Twitter rolled out a new version of its profile page, complete with a big 1500 x 500 pixel Facebook-esque header image - a large banner that spans the whole width of the page, ripe for customizing with your own design. How you choose to fill this space is up to you, but tactics similar to Facebook - simple branding, highlighting promotions, featuring customers, etc. are a few of the most common strategies. To edit your header image, click the "Edit profile" button on your page and then "Change your header image."

Create a custom Twitter background image
In previous versions of Twitter for desktop, users could upload a custom design that spanned the whole width of the a profile page'

background. Although this is no longer possible on the "home" page of a Twitter profile, you *can* still insert a background image to appear when someone clicks on an individual tweet to view it (and the conversation attached to it) on a separate page. Although the eyeballs this portion of your Twitter profile's branding will be considerably less than that your cover photo, the people that *do* click individual tweets are, by nature, probably more interested in what you have to say, so the background customization here might appeal to them more than the average Twitter user.

Free Twitter header and background templates

The way that your Twitter header and background images appear differs on different desktop resolutions. To make creating the perfect Twitter header and background designs as easy as possible (i.e. to avoid their most important elements being weirdly cropped or hidden by the profile photo or feed), I have created two free templates for use with Adobe Photoshop or GIMP. Once you have downloaded the templates, follow the instructions, then save the files as a .png ready for upload to Twitter. Grab your free template via the link in the *Free Social Media Templates* chapter of this book.

Should you post your Tweets to Facebook?

Your Twitter profile settings include the option to send your tweets automatically to the wall of your Facebook business Page. Whether you decide to use this is personal preference - but my advice would be to avoid it, for several reasons. Chances are that you are going to be posting on Twitter much more regularly than Facebook, so you risk the chance of spamming (and upsetting) your Facebook fans. Secondly, you want people to be fans of you on Twitter AND Facebook, and to be able to offer both audiences a unique, valuable experience. They won't come to Twitter if they can get it all on Facebook. And lastly, but perhaps most importantly, automated posts (whether written by hand or produced by a bot) are never received as well as a post that is individually crafted for its intended audience. The ways you communicate with your Twitter and Facebook audiences are different, so it's best to keep them separate.

Promote and sell with the Twitter widget and Tweet button
Twitter has its own equivalent of the Facebook "Like" box, which shows a live preview of your Twitter stream's latest activity, along with a "Follow" button and a box for users to tweet to you. Create yours at https://twitter.com/settings/widgets and embed it prominently on your website to attract new followers.

To increase website page views and to drive sales, you can also grab an official Twitter "Tweet" button to place above or below each of your blog posts, or next to products on your website (when someone tweets from the button, it will be seen by many of their followers who will be encouraged to take a look). Set one up at this link: https://about.twitter.com/resources/buttons. When you set your "Tweet" button up, make sure to check the box to show the tweet count (the more times a post or product link has been tweeted, the more likely someone else is to share it too), and include a hashtag relevant to your brand that will automatically be added to the auto-generated tweet. However, you'll want to switch up the "Share URL" and "Tweet text" options depending whether the button will sit on a blog post or product page.

For blog posts: Set the Share URL option to use the page URL, use the title of the page for the tweet text, then enter your username into the via box. An example might read: *"How to Use Snapchat Stories to Captivate Fans http://www.andrewmacarthy.com/-captivate-fans-with-snapchat-stories #snapchatmarketing via @andrewmacarthy."* The long URL will automatically be shortened by Twitter.

For product pages: Set the Share URL option to use the page URL, but customize the tweet text to read like the sharer is tweeting about the item personally, and not in over-promotional manner, e.g. *"I love these stripy Craesa sneakers from Aldo #aldoshoes http://www.aldoshoes.com/women/shoes/trainers/30189991-craesa/16."* Again, the long URL will be automatically shortened upon tweeting.

Encourage tweets and social sharing using Tweet This
Short, helpful, and inspirational quotes are a brilliant way to market you and your business on Twitter, and one of the coolest ways to implement this strategy is via the free Tweet This website at http://dashburst.com/tweet-this/.

Here's how it works:
1. Enter a quote from your blog or website that you want others to tweet.
2. Click the "Generate Tweet Link" button to create a custom link URL and embed code.
3. Share the link and/or get the embed code.

If you imagine the following quote is a part of one of my blog posts or a page on my website, the final result from Tweet This might look something like: *"Consistency is one of the key strategies to rocking your social media strategy via @500socialmedia [Tweet This]"*, where ["Tweet This"] is a clickable link that opens up the user's Twitter account, pre-populates the status update box with my chosen quote, and is ready for them to share with all of their followers instantly. Notice how I included my @username to add an element of attribution, which might also gain me some new custom.

Another strategy for Tweet This involves using it on the "Confirmation" page that loads after a purchase on your website has taken place, as an opportunity to encourage someone who has just purchased to share their excitement about the transaction, e.g. *"I just bought a copy of 500 Social Media Marketing Tips - I'll be a pro in no time! #socialmediamarketing [product link]."* Make sure to include a link back to your main store page and a unique hashtag for tracking.

Concoct the perfect tweet, but avoid text speak
Spelling, punctuation and grammar all count, especially when you only have 140 characters to communicate your point in a single tweet. Practice writing the perfect tweet, and always double-check for errors. While it might be tempting to use text speak to cram as much as you can into Twitter's 140-character limit, doing so is at best unprofessional, and at worst makes your tweets unreadable.

Don't exceed the tweet limit
Wherever possible, do not allow your Twitter statuses to spill over into multiple tweets (i.e. over 140 characters), as this makes it confusing for your followers to keep track of what you are trying to say, especially if they have a really busy Twitter feed, where your updates may appear sandwiched between tweets appearing from other people that they follow.

If there is no way that you can keep a Twitter update to 140 characters or fewer, consider using a service like TwitLonger (http://www.twitlonger.com/) as a workaround. This site allows you to type as long a message as you like. When you submit the message, it will be sent out to your followers using your Twitter account. The first portion will be visible, then a URL will be displayed to allow followers to click through to read the full message at the Twitlonger website. An example tweet might read:

"This tweet is going to exceed the 140-character limit set by Twitter, so I am using TwitLonger.com (cont) tl.gd/n_1rjtjti"

Tweets: aim for quality not quantity
Don't post tweets every minute of the day, spamming your followers' feeds and annoying them enough to unfollow you - be sparing. In fact, more than two or three tweets an hour has been shown to decrease engagement.

Share links to useful content, shorten and track with bit.ly
To help grow your number of followers, post links to useful and interesting content (whether your own or by others) that is likely to be retweeted. Use Google Alerts to be notified of fun, fresh, and relevant content for your Twitter feed and followers, and use 'Tweet This' buttons to get it to them fast. While it's good to share interesting content with your followers, make sure you know what's in it before tweeting - i.e. always read it first! The last thing you want to do is upset your audience.

If you will be including a link to your own content within a tweet, always shorten it beforehand using a site like bit.ly. Twitter will ordinarily shorten links automatically, but using bit.ly also allows you to customize them for neatness and analyze the click-through rate, which is great for seeing what kind of content resonates best with your followers. When using a shortened link on Twitter, double check that it works before posting. One broken link might mean a customer never clicks on your URLs again.

Use hashtags to group tweets and encourage engagement
Use #hashtags to group tweets of the same kind and to highlight your message. Top-trending hashtags appear on Twitter's home page, and can easily be found via Twitter search. Tweets that include hashtags have been proven to receive twice as much engagement as those without, so their usage is vital. Don't include

more than one or two hashtags per tweet, as it can get confusing for followers; engagement with tweets that include more than two hashtags tails off considerably, research shows.

Short hashtags work best. #ilovechocolatecakeandeatiteveryday - a hashtag like this is difficult to read and eats up precious characters within your tweet. In addition, use legible formatting. Symbols don't work too well, and capitalizing words helps make hashtags a bit more readable, e.g. #BigSale rather than #bigsale.

Here are some more important benefits of using hashtags on Twitter and other social networks:

To find new fans
Use custom-made hashtags to bolster your brand identity and location, such as #billysburgers #BerwynIL respectively, especially useful when new customers click to learn more about you.

To promote live events and other ad campaigns
Fans of your brand love to show off what they're up to with friends via text, image, and video updates. If you are holding an event or launching a new promotion, make sure these fan updates are tied together strongly by publicizing and encouraging the use of a representative hashtag before, during, and after.

To gather feedback and measure ROI
More than ever, users of Twitter and other social networks are tagging their updates with "emotion" hashtags, e.g. "Had an awesome meal at Betty's Grill today! #stuffed #bestburgersever." Whether the sentiments are good or bad, they can often give you a deeper insight into your brand image than you imagined. In addition, either manually, or via services like Hashtracking.com, you can use hashtags to help track the success of a campaign.

In summary, people who see a hashtag tend to click on it, explore it, use it in their own posts or even check out the person or brand that tweeted it, according to a 2013 study carried out by RadiumOne, so I would definitely recommend including them in your updates where relevant.

Tweet your top content several times, schedule for ease

Twitter feeds are dynamic and fast-moving, and people also check them at different times of the day, so make sure your top links aren't missed; post them, under different guises, several times a day. Unlike Facebook users who are likely to scroll through their News Feeds and notice if you are posting the same information several times a day, the speed at which messages on Twitter are shared means that users aren't likely to notice (or care) as much, so the protocol here is a bit more relaxed. If you produce a lot of valuable "evergreen" blog content, i.e. that which will remain useful no matter its age, use a service like Buffer (www.bufferapp.com) to schedule and automatically post tweets linking to this content periodically. Here's a free tutorial, which shows how you can upload in bulk, too: http://bit.ly/scheduleoldblogtweets

Pin important Twitter posts

If you want to spotlight a particularly important tweet, you can pin it to the top of your feed for extra visibility - all subsequent posts will appear below it. On the desktop version of Twitter, click on the three little dots underneath a tweet and choose "pin to your profile page."

Leave space to encourage retweet comments

If you want your content to be retweeted (i.e. re-posted on someone else's feed to their followers), first of all you need to make sure it is worth retweeting! As lots of people like to add their own comments to retweets via a program like TweetDeck, I recommend that your original tweet -if possible - does not exceed 120 characters or so. That leaves a retweeter 20 characters to add any additional comment without exceeding the maximum length of 140 characters.

Balance tweets, replies and RTs - and don't over-promote
Too much of one thing isn't great for balance where Twitter is concerned, so be sure to tweet, @reply, and retweet in equal measure. Like all social networks, there's nothing worse than simply promoting your own wares and nothing else - do it sparingly. Got a happy customer tweeting you? Encourage them to share their happiness further, with @replies that ask for photos or videos of the product or service you provided, which you can then retweet onto your own wall. Keep in mind that @messages, when used at the very beginning of a tweet, only appear in the feeds of those who follow both you and the person you are messaging. If used in the middle of a tweet, all of your followers will see it. Use this information to help separate the tweets you want just your followers to see, and those you want everyone to see.

Retweeting people you hope to build relationships with is one good strategy: pay special attention to just a few peers who post great tweets and retweet them every now and again (use Twitter directories such as twello and Justtweetit to find your targets). Additionally, make your followers and customers feel special by retweeting their positive posts about you, or by including their comments in a blog post or in testimonials on your website. If you have space, add your opinion too (programs like TweetDeck allow you to add to and edit a RT before sending it). While it might sound counter-productive at first, promoting other tweeters' messages more than your own is good for karma, and will sow the seed for reciprocal action later on down the line.

Respond to @mentions and DMs quickly

Whenever you receive notification of an @mention of your brand, be sure to respond as soon as possible. A lot of the bigger businesses don't, and it hits their credibility hard. Also keep a close eye on any direct messages (DMs) you receive, and use them to respond to customers quickly and efficiently. Respond to negative tweets even more quickly! The longer you leave a negative tweet lingering, the more people will see it, assuming that you don't really care about your customers. You can only send a direct message to a user who is following you, and you can only receive direct messages from users you follow, so facilitate this beforehand.

Show appreciation with favorites

For a more subtle way to thank your followers for their kind words about your business, favorite a tweet by clicking the star icon next to it. Not only is favoriting tweets an easy way to collate customer testimonials - or 'save' a tweet that you want to think about or investigate before replying to (they appear in the Favorites menu of your Twitter profile for easy reference) - but a user is also notified when one of their tweets is favorited. Different to retweeting, however, is that this notification is not shared publicly – only with the individual to whom it applies – so it looks a little less like you are tooting your own horn… not that it's a bad thing to do very occasionally!

Thank your newest followers, and follow back

When someone follows you, be sure to @reply to thank them if you have the time, or retweet something interesting from their feed - it's a good icebreaker at the start of what, hopefully, will be a long relationship. Don't be tempted to use a tool to auto-thank users who follow, or send them promotional material. As a first impression, it doesn't go down well at all. I usually say something like this to initiate conversation: *"Hey, @newfollower, thanks for following! How are you doing today? Andrew."*

Use images to drive engagement, as a text replacement, and to tease offers

In research carried out by Hubspot in 2013, tweets that included photos were found to be significantly more likely to be retweeted than those without. The study also revealed that tweets containing pictures uploaded directly to the site are nearly twice as likely to be retweeted than those from external sources such as Instagram - the latter display as plain text links rather than appearing directly within the feed.

While images and uploaded to Twitter appear within the feed, they do not always display in their entirety. To stop the feed becoming too cluttered, photos over a certain height are reduced to a letterbox-sized preview window that a user must click to expand and view the image in full. Rather than a limitation, view this feature as an opportunity to market to your Twitter audience in brand new ways, like posting "banner ad" images designed to display so that they will not be cropped, and "expand to reveal" offers that encourage people to click to see more. Think about the ways you can use images on Twitter in conjunction with (or largely instead of) a text update to communicate a message to your audience that might otherwise be difficult in just 140 characters. As Twitter is specific about which portion of an uploaded image shows in the news feed by default, I have created a template that will help you get it right every time. Grab your free template via the link in the Free Social Media Templates chapter of this book.

Upload multiple images and tag them to boost engagement

Clear evidence that Twitter is keen to bolster the use of images on the site arrived in April 2014, when the ability to attach up to four images to a tweet (previously limited to just one) was introduced. Multiple images display as a collage of four rectangular images on all devices, and also in embedded tweets. Brands are already taking

71

advantage of these collages to spell out a single message across the four separate images, provide simple step-by-step tutorials, or using multiple photos to tell the story of an event in the life of their company.

Along with this update comes the ability to tag up to 10 people, e.g. customers, contest winners, business associates, etc. in each image. The people who are tagged will receive a notification to let them know, so do take advantage of this as a way to encourage engagement and start conversations centered on your posts. To top it all off, the characters used to tag usernames in Twitter images will not deplete any the original 140 character space for the accompanying text. To tag people in a photo, select it once uploaded and type their name or username into the "Who's in this photo?" box. When the tweet is published, the usernames of the tagged people will appear next to it as live, clickable links.

For a deeper insight into how you can use both images and videos on Twitter to provide great content, check out the Facebook Tips, Instagram Tips, YouTube Tips, and Vine Tips chapters of this book.

Hold a competition on Twitter
Twitter is a great platform to hold a competition on, to encourage views and interaction with your page, or link to an external source. Entry requirements can be as simple as asking your followers to retweet something that you have written or @replying to answer a question. If you run a competition, don't ask users to DM you the answer to a question: it shuts off promotion of the competition to vast numbers of users who won't see others tweeting to you in Twitter's search.

Real-time offers and Twitter-specific codes
Offer your Twitter followers special coupons and timely discounts to help raise your brand's reputation. If you want to measure sales

made specifically through Twitter, tweet a tracking code only to your followers and be sure to ask for it during the transaction. e.g. TWEET20. As an aside, you can use different codes on each of your social media platforms; if you request these when a customer books, you can easily track which platform is the most effective. Do remember to keep a note of which you used, and where!

Take orders over Twitter

Why not try taking orders or bookings over Twitter? If you want to give it a go but are worried it will clutter up your main profile, you can just as easily create a separate Twitter account and dedicate that one for taking orders.

Meet up with followers and promote your Twitter feed

Find ways to take a step beyond Twitter relationships by meeting your followers and followees in real life - great for taking networking to that next step. At business events, display tweets with the event #hashtag on a big screen using services such as twitterfall.com or visibletweets.com, and tweet to your followers about the experience while you're there.

Host Twitter chats for engagement and authority building

Twitter chats - live, structured conversations between users on Twitter - are a really effective way to engage with and build stronger relationships with your audience, and also encourage new people to follow you. Set a date and time, a unique hashtag (so that others can follow along and join in more easily), and encourage interaction by promoting the event well in advance.

Many brands host weekly Twitter chats as a way to build authority within their niche, promote their products and services, and to grow their professional network by interacting with peers. Before you jump in and start your own, I'd recommend searching for and observing a couple of existing Twitter chats within your industry to familiarize yourself with how they work, and to get a feel for whether they might be suitable for your own business objectives. Sites like http://tweetreports.com/twitter-chat-schedule/ feature tons of examples for you to choose from (or you could simply search the web for "[your keyword] + twitter chat), while http://www.tchat.io/ allows you to easily follow and reply in real-time to tweets that include a specific hashtag, i.e. the one uses for your chat!

Use Embeddable tweets

Use embeddable tweets to take a tweet or a conversation and post it on your website or in a blog post. You can use this feature to share your Twitter conversation with a larger audience.

1. Locate a tweet on Twitter.com that you want to embed.
2. Hover your mouse over the tweet and click 'Expand'.
3. Click 'Details'.
4. Click 'Embed this Tweet'.
5. Click inside the HTML code box to highlight the code. Copy the HTML code (CTRL+C or Command+C) and paste it as an HTML element into your website or blog.

Creative uses for Embedded tweets

- Tweets can be a great source of customer testimonials for your business, particularly if you embed them onto your website or blog.
- Do you host business events? Embed the invitation tweet in a list of upcoming events on your website.
- Embed tweets from other people into your blog posts. Embedded tweets allow your readers to connect with new people and jump into the Twitter conversation right from your blog.
- Embed part of a Twitter conversation (one that has inspired a blog post) into your blog and reach more people than the original Twitter conversation.

- Embed a tweet of a glowing customer comment or add a tweet about an upcoming event in your email signature, to help seal deals and promote your activity.

Use Twitter Search to discover and connect with customers
Use Twitter Search to find people who have mentioned your business name, website address, etc. and interact with them. Target your search by location and date in the Advanced Twitter search (https://twitter.com/search-advanced) for more localized and time-specific results, and use keywords within quotation marks and the minus symbol (-) to omit results with unwanted keywords, e.g. "'Paula's Prom Dresses -tiara'" - any other Boolean search technique will also work. One cool strategy is to use keywords associated with your business to find the problems which people are tweeting about, and target the issues that your business can solve. Pair your company's name or related ideas with words like "bad" or "sucks" to find people complaining, and do the same using common misspellings of your brand name, @mentions and hashtags to catch as many people as possible. On a similar note, make sure to filter search results to "Show All", not just the "Top Tweets." You never know, one single helpful tweet could lead to customer loyalty that lasts for years.

Before February 2013, Twitter search results only displayed tweets going back about a week, but this period is now lengthening all the time. Twitter search won't display every tweet mentioning your keywords or hashtag that has ever existed, but it will look at a variety of types of engagement, such as favorites, retweets and clicks, to determine which Tweets to show. Although some mentions might be weeks or months old, it is still worth retweeting or engaging with them, as you never know where a dormant mention may lead.

Save Twitter searches

Use the 'Save search' feature on Twitter to quickly access regular searches that you make, such as those searching for mentions of your brand name and keywords related to it.

To save a Twitter search:
1. Type your search query into the search box at the top of the page and hit return.
2. Click on the gear icon and select 'Save search' from the drop down menu.

To revisit a saved search:
1. Click anywhere in the search box at the top of the page. A list of your saved searches will appear below the search box.
2. Click on the saved search to revisit results for that query.

Search and 'steal' customers from the competition
If you have a local competitor, search for tweets mentioning their business name as well as your own. I wouldn't wholeheartedly recommend replying to the tweets you find, because it could come across as too being too desperate or forward, but just knowing what is being said about your competition can be enough to give you ideas to help you up your own game and give you a competitive edge. If you *do* decide to respond to tweets mentioning your competitors (if the rival firm doesn't ever reply, for example), be helpful and conversational with no put-downs and no hard selling. Hopefully your good grace will get the customer in question to switch allegiances.

Create Twitter Lists to segment tweets
Twitter Lists allow you to easily organize and view the content most worth reading from the people you follow. Tweets from people in your Twitter lists appear in a separate feed, which can allow you to filter out a lot of the 'noise' on the platform. Examples of groups of people you can sort into Twitter lists

include customers, potential customers, people with whom you interact most, professional contacts and people who inspire you. Follow lists created by others too, as it is a subtle way to get others to find your own profile.

How to create a Twitter List:
1. Click on the cog icon at the top of your Twitter profile and choose 'Lists'.
2. On the page that loads, click the 'Create list' button.
3. Give your list a name and description, e.g. Business Influencers, and choose whether you want to make it public or private. When you create a public list, list members see when you add or delete them from the list, and any member of Twitter can choose to follow your list. When you create a private list, people are not notified when they appear on it; only you can see the list's tweet timeline.
4. Search for people to add to your list by username, real name, or business or brand name.
You can also add people direct from the page which shows all of the people you are following. On the 'head and shoulders' icon next to the name of the person you want to add to a list, choose the 'Add or remove from lists...' option and select the list you want to add them to.

Use custom timelines to organize and curate key tweets
Twitter introduced custom timelines in November 2013, a feature that affords you more control over how tweets are organized and delivered. Unlike the default Twitter timeline, custom timelines are ones that you create, name, and add tweets to. This means that when the conversation around an event or topic blows up on Twitter, you can create a timeline that surfaces what you believe to be the most noteworthy and relevant tweets. Custom timelines are public and have their own unique URL, making them easy to share with others. They can be embedded onto your website, too! Use

custom timelines to help people easily find the latest information about fast-moving events like product launches, flash sales, business conferences, and lots more.

To create a custom timeline, download and install the free Tweetdeck program (a brilliant tool for managing your Twitter presence, by the way), then add a new column of type "Custom timeline". To add a new column you can use the add icon "+" in the sidebar or the keyboard shortcut "A". To add a Tweet to a custom timeline, drag it with the move icon and drop it on the custom timeline column that you would like to populate. The share menu for custom timelines includes a link to generate the code to create an embedded custom timeline; just paste this code wherever on your website you want your custom timeline to appear.

Consider a profile dedicated to customer service

Depending on your company's resources and levels of Twitter interaction, you may want to consider opening a Twitter account dedicated only to responding to negative queries from customers. The idea here is that you can use your brand's main Twitter handle to focus on positive engagement, sharing valuable content, and posting the odd marketing message - leaving your secondary account open to host conversations with unhappy customers. If this is something you intend to do, be sure to make clear which account customers should tweet to with complaints by placing the @username and an explanation on your website, pamphlets, and in your main Twitter account's Bio or background design.

Switch to a personal Twitter account for pressing matters

For the very most pressing matters, switch to your personal Twitter account to deal with customers who require special treatment to keep them on side. It will show the customer that you really care about them and, perhaps more importantly, it will protect your brand image from a storm of controversy away from your company's Twitter account.

Handle acute problems with direct messages

If lots of people are asking the same question on Twitter in a short amount of time, due to an acute problem, use direct messaging (DMs) to reply to them and prevent clogging your news feed with @replies. To prevent further negative tweets flying in your direction, post one public tweet to explain the situation, so that it can be seen prominently on your news feed.

Paid advertising on Twitter

While Twitter advertising doesn't have the same depth as Facebook's tools, it can still be a very powerful strategy in helping you reach your audience, and it won't break the bank either, with bid amounts as low as $1.50 for promoted tweet engagements and $3 per follower. Let's take a look at the types of Twitter advertising available to you:

Promoted Tweets

Choose a specific tweet to promote and it will appear right at the top of your target audience's Twitter feed. Promoted tweets can also appear at the top of Twitter search results.

Twitter allows you to target users based on keywords that users search or tweet about, their location, and their interests. In the case of the latter, you can target people with interests similar to the followers of any Twitter username you enter, so you can even target ads to display in front of your competitor's followers. Once your targeting option is chosen, you'll be able to manually select the tweets you want to promote or let Twitter automatically select your five most engaging recent tweets for further exposure.

Note: If you are trying to achieve specific goals, such as advertising your latest product launch or the hosting of an event coming up in the near future, it is better to compose a custom tweet for it using the Promote a New Tweet option.

Promoted Accounts
With promoted accounts, your Twitter username, profile photo and a Follow button will appear as a suggestion in strategic spots across Twitter on desktop and mobile, such as the Who to Follow box. The targeting options here are more limited than that of Promoted Posts, but it is a simple method for gaining exposure for your account and business, and attracting new followers in the process.

Lead Generation Cards
Lead generation cards are tweets that allow you, directly on Twitter, to collect the names and email addresses of potential leads or customers and add them to your mailing list. When you tweet about something, e.g. a free guide to laying amazing turf every time when someone joins your mailing list, a "card" will be attached to the bottom of the tweet with space for a promotional image, boxes for users to type in their name and e-mail address, and a button for them to join your mailing list and download your guide instantly.

Twitter advertising tips
- To begin setting up a Twitter ad campaign, visit https://ads.twitter.com/
- Target your ad campaigns precisely to reach the most relevant audience, gain the most conversions, and save money.
- A/B test your promoted material to see which performs the best and keep tweaking until you find the optimum setup.
- Set up Conversion Tracking within the Twitter advertising dashboard as a way to measure return on investment.

Google+ Tips:
Plus One Your Marketing Strategy

Google+ (or Google Plus) is the search giant's answer to Facebook. It might not have the numbers of its rival, but its user base is still huge. As of February 2014, it had over 540 million active users. Due to Google's dominance of search on the web, it is very useful for businesses to maintain a Google+ presence. At present, there is no easier way to increase visibility of your content on Google search than to encourage comments, shares, and +1s (the social network's equivalent of Facebook "likes") on your Google+ account. Think of Google+ as the glue that holds all Google products (Gmail, Google Docs, YouTube, etc.) together; it is socializing the whole Google experience. As a marketer, it is useful to consider this idea, and differentiate it from something like Facebook, which is much more of a singular destination site. Use the following tips to build, brand, improve search engine ranking and form relationships using Google+.

Get a business page, not a profile page

As with Facebook, make sure you create a Google+ business page for your brand rather than another personal profile. To start, visit http://www.google.com/+/business/ and follow the step-by-step instructions to begin the set up. If you already have a personal Google+ profile, choose the 'Pages' option from the sidebar on your profile page (it may be hidden under the 'More...' menu) instead. Even with a business page, don't completely neglect your personal profile. It'll come in handy where the Google Authorship scheme is concerned (explained later on), especially if you are a blogger.

Grab a Google+ custom URL

In October 2013, Google+ began to give Google+ users with accounts in good standing, 30+ days old, with 10 or more followers, and featuring a profile photo, a pre-selected custom URL for their profile or business page - one that is much shorter and more memorable than that assigned by default when an account is first created. When you meet this criteria, a notification will appear at the top of your Google+ page or profile. To get started, click the "Get a custom URL button" to *or* the "Get" link in your Google+ About section. Select the URL you want to use for your Page from those available - there could be just one or several - and click "Change URL". You may need to verify your information to continue. Once approved, the URL you selected will be permanently linked to your Google+ page or Profile and you can't request to change it, so make sure you are happy.

Upload a compelling cover image, grab my free template
Use your Google+ cover image to express your brand image, tell people where you are, showcase new products, advertise upcoming events, or for whatever you like, really. As of November 2013, the recommended size is 1080 pixels × 608 pixels, and the smallest image size you are allowed to upload is 480 pixels × 270 pixels. By uploading the larger size, you ensure that your cover will be seen in its best light on mobiles and desktops.

Free Google+ cover photo template
To make creating and optimizing your Google+ cover photo as easy as possible, I have created a free template for use with Adobe Photoshop or GIMP. Download the template, follow the instructions within it to insert your design, then save the file as a .png ready for upload to Google+. Grab your free template via the link in the *Free Social Media Templates* chapter of this book.

Add a circular profile photo or a transparent logo

The Google+ profile image switched from a square to a circle in March 2013. Its minimum size is 250 × 250 pixels, and this will be scaled down to 104 × 104 pixels when re-sized. If you have a square company logo, you might find it tricky to get it to fit fully *inside* Google+'s profile photo circle on your page, even with the cropping and sizing tools that present themselves when you upload. The trick here is to upload your profile image as a .png file with a transparent background. Upon upload, drag the cropping edges right to the corners so that the while image will show on your business page. If your image still doesn't look right at this stage, click on it from your profile and choose More -> Auto Enhance -> off from the menu at the top.

Add a compelling tagline

In your 'About' section, Google+ allows you to add a tagline to appear underneath your Page's main business name. The tagline acts like an elevator pitch to visitors, will appear as the description when somebody shares your page, and as the first sentence when your Google+ page is found in Google search. Keep it short, snappy, descriptive and keyword-rich, or as a message to explain who you are and what you and your business is all about. Check out a few examples from these well-known names for inspiration:

Yahoo! News
"The official Google+ page for Yahoo! News. All stories are hand-picked by the Y! News team."

Volkswagen
"Take a look around, kick the tires, and ask questions to get to know our community."

ESPN
"We +1 Sports"

Max out the About section with keywords and links

Fill out your Google+ profile's About section completely. Do not leave any field empty, as this section may be the first port of call for a potential customer. Focus on using keywords you want to rank highly on in search, and the keywords your customers are using. Of course, don't just list them or shoehorn them in, make the text nice to read. The same goes for your page posts: carefully consider which keywords best represent your online brand and pepper them throughout your content. This will make you more visible to customers, both in Google+ and Google's main web search.

Use the Recommended Links area of your About section to add links to your blog, social profiles, local listings and review sites you want to promote. As Google+ is tied very closely to Google web search, take advantage by posting plenty of links to your business in your Introduction, and Contact Info sections of your profile, too - every link back helps. To spread the word of your Google+ page beyond your fans, ask your employees to set up individual Google+ profiles (if they haven't already) and get them add the URL to your business page in their Links section.

Add a +1 button and Google+ badges to your website

If you write a blog, be sure to add a +1 button widget to your posts, so that your fans can share your content on Google+ easily. Just search for "Google+ button" or grab the embed code from the following link:
https://developers.google.com/+/web/+1button/

The Google+ badge is the equivalent to the Facebook "Like" box in that it lets readers follow you on Google+ without leaving your site. In addition, however, it also has benefits within search results. When you embed the Google+ badge for pages on your site, an active Follow widget will show up next to your website's listing in

Google search results. To install the Google+ Badge, simply search online for "Google+ Badge" or visit https://developers.google.com/+/web/badge/. Choose your page from the drop-down menu, select your badge type, then copy and paste the embed code onto your blog or website.

Participate in, and manage, Circles

As true for all social networks, make sure you interact often with your fans. Google+'s Circles feature lets you users segment your followers and people you follow. This means that, as a business, you can send out select status updates to select people. For example, you can organize your Circles into current customers, prospective customers, new customers, influential peers, etc. Concentrate on creating circles on a micro level, and make sure to nurture your relationship with them. Send out exclusive content, interact directly, start a hangout with just one circle, etc.

Only circle those people who enrich your networking and add value to the Google+ experience - don't settle for just anyone; define your own criteria and stick to it. One of the best ways to find people is to combine your business page and personal page. Through your personal page, you can use the Google + shared circle databases to begin conversations with people relevant to your industry.

On the flip side, getting fans to like and circle your page on Google+ is crucial to be able to easily disseminate your posts to them. However, you cannot jump into people's circle, they must circle you. To get people to circle you, refer to your Google+ business page once you have engaged in a conversation with them, whether it be on Google+ or elsewhere.

Share top content, boost your SEO

Your Google+ audience may differ to those on Facebook and Twitter, so get to know them by asking questions, polling, sharing great and relevant content, and interacting. Posting great content on Google+ does more than reach out to your circles and other users — it also "markets" to search engines. Anytime you post content to Google+, Google immediately indexes it, giving you faster exposure to new viewers. When you share a link to an article on your Google+ page (whether it is your own content or someone else's) write the first sentence of the post mindfully with relevant keywords and phrases. The first sentence is of a post makes up part of the title tag in search results and can affect its ranking. If you notice that your post isn't getting much attention, try editing the text you used to see if that improves things. The longer a piece of content exists, the longer it's in the index of Google, so as people continue to search and interact with it, it will continue to show up near the top of search results. What's more, your content is more likely to appear in your contacts' online searches, thanks to Google's personalized results.

Embed Google+ Posts on your website
Like Twitter and Facebook, Google+ allows you to lift posts you publish and embed them onto your website or blog, which can help to give your content an extra lease of life and boost its engagement. When someone encounters the Google+ embedded post on your site, they can +1, comment, or follow you, all without leaving your site.

How to embed a Google+ post
1. On Google+, move your cursor over the right corner of a post to reveal a down arrow. Click the arrow to expand the post options and select "Embed post."
2. A text box containing HTML/Javascript code will appear. Copy and paste the code in the location of your article where you'd like to display the post.

Sign up for Google Authorship to boost blog visibility

The Google Authorship program for your personal Google+ account is Google's way of authenticating the content you produce and accepting it as a source of high quality work, which in turn can help to build your authority and influence. One of its many benefits is having a photo appear next to your blog posts in search results, which helps readers spot your content at a glance and creates a visual bond between you and them.

Google Authorship benefits:
- Higher click through rates on search results, because they stand out more.
- More traffic to your Google+ profile, which is linked in the search result.
- More traffic to other content authored by you, via the "More by" link in the search result.

How to register for Google Authorship
1. Upload a high quality headshot as your personal profile photo on Google+ and make sure your profile information is filled out in its entirety.
2. Go to plus.google.com/authorship, sign up with your email and click on the verification link sent to you.

If you contribute to multiple blogs, you might prefer the following solution, which will link content from numerous sites to your Google+ profile. Here's what to do:

1. In the author bio or "about the author" section at the end of each of your blog posts, include a link to your Google+ profile with a "?rel=author" tag (without the speech marks) added to the end of it, e.g.:
https://plus.google.com/116769735259794960589?rel=author

2. Visit the About section of your Google+ profile. Under the "Contributor to" section, paste a link to your author page for each blog that you contribute to.

Use pictures and video for higher engagement
Much more powerful than text are images and video, and they work incredibly well on Google+, dominating the "What's hot and recommended" section under the Explore tab. Be sure to use images to your advantage by implementing the strategies for images detailed throughout this book, and the fact that Google+ does not crop or resize uploaded photos, so that they always retain their visual impact. In your Profile settings, make all photos public, downloadable and showing geo-location for as transparent and shareable an experience as possible. One of the benefits of sharing YouTube videos to Google+ is that when you post a YouTube video to Google+, users can view and comment on the media within their feed, and these comments *also* appear on your YouTube video.

If you want to take image and video enhancement a step further, Google+'s Auto Awesome feature allows you to create GIF-style media for your page using photos, videos or both. To begin, download the Google+ mobile app, then enable Auto Awesome from the Camera Settings menu. After snapping or recording on mobile, upload the content to Google+ and shortly afterwards your animation will materialize.

Edit and format posts on Google+
Google+ allows you to edit existing posts any time after they have been published. Be sure to edit if you make a mistake, or use it as an opportunity to add extra information. To edit a post on Google+, click on the arrow in the top-right hand corner of the content in question and choose "Edit post" from the drop-down menu. You can also add emboldening, italics, and strikethrough to

your Google+ post headlines and within posts themselves to highlight key words and phrases. Use the format *text* to embolden; _text_ to italicize; and -text- to strike through a word or phrase.

Use Mentions and hashtags

As with Twitter and Facebook, @mentions and hashtags are important on Google+, both in tagging other users in your posts and grouping related content. To hyperlink someone's name in your posts, type "+" or "@" and then his or her name. Hashtags also work on Google+ - take a look ways you can benefit from using hashtags in the Twitter chapter of this book.

Hunt for prospects and brand ambassadors on Google+

As with Twitter, you can Boolean search techniques on Google+ to find people who are talking about your brand, services, or products using the search bar at the top of the site. To begin, enter keywords, as well as hashtags that are related to your brand or niche, then filter your search by content type (posts, photos, most recent mentions, etc.) to find mentions with the most potential. Utilize searches as a means to discover potential customers (e.g. people with problems you can solve or desires you can meet) or existing brand ambassadors (people saying nice things about you), and target them to build strong, long-lasting relationships that will convert into further sharing of your content, leading them to influence the emergence of new customers and conversions further on down the line.

To organize and simplify this process, after performing a search, browse the results on show, and add people to separate Circles for "potential" and "existing loyal customers" based on what you see, then begin to interact by offering +1s, commenting on posts, and imparting useful advice with these individuals. In time, you'll begin to notice which targets have been most receptive to your approaches, and they can be moved from your "potential brand ambassador" Circle to the one for "existing loyal customers". Then, the process repeats from the beginning.

Advanced prospect hunting on Google+

Hashtags are particularly useful for prospect hunting on Google+ as they allow you to deepen your investigation to find and interact with new brand ambassadors. When you search using hashtags, the results will show the hashtag you searched for, as well as related hashtags. You can click on the hashtag(s) to flip the search result "cards" and find more related content posted by other Google+ users. After you flip a "card", browse the related results and make note of the level of activity attached to each person's post - the more engagement they receive, the more influential they are likely to be.

Other ways to find brand ambassadors
- Browse Google+ communities: most allow you to join immediately.
- Snoop at your competitors' pages: If they have the Who Has Them in Circles feature on show, identify if any of those people may fit for your brand and place them in your Circle designated for potential influencers.
- Google web search: Whack in a selection of queries that your target audience would use to find you and focus on results tagged with Google Authorship to reach the Google+ profiles of prime candidates. Make sure you use a private/incognito window to return non-personalized search results.

When you spot a person whose posts has a reasonable amount of engagement and you would like to pursue, click the little arrow in the upper-right corner of the card and choose "View Ripples" from the menu that appears. Ripples is a unique and interactive tool provided by Google+ to measure the 'virality' of public posts on the site. The larger the circle of a sharer, the more relative influence they have. After that, as in the basic model of prospect hunting, it's a case of initiating friendly interaction through +1s, comments, and sharing valuable content to foster stronger and more loyal relationships, and getting fans to spread the word about you on Google+ and beyond simply because you are so awesome!

Targeting prospects on Google+ using email

To push your Google+ prospect hunting and marketing to the nth degree, you can experiment with sending brand ambassadors an email containing a special invitation. Construct a non-spammy offer that fills the unique needs of these customers - something like an exclusive look at your upcoming product, or a ambassadors-only Google Hangout Q&A; you really don't want to turn them off by emailing them out of the blue, so make it worth their while! In the same email, invite the recipients to subscribe to your mailing list to be notified the next time you have something exciting to share. Those people that take this extra step are the real cream of the crop; true lovers and evangelists for your brand who you now have a fully-consented direct line of communication to. Identify these fans and place them into a special new Circle on Google+ reserved for only your most passionate customers. I cannot stress this enough: be *very* careful with this strategy, as one wrong move could put a lot of people off you very fast, especially if the email is unsolicited.

How to send an email to Google+ users

Begin composing a Gmail e-mail on a desktop computer, and start typing the name of the person you want to contact in the "To" field. If there's a match in your Google+ Circles (and that person hasn't opted out of receiving emails from Google+ users), their name and photo pop up for you to select.

Use Google+ Communities to engage and gather feedback

Launched in late 2012, the Google+ Communities tab gives your customers a place to gather with one another and discuss your products and brand offering. As a business tool, it is an invaluable resource as it allows you to get feedback and engage with your customers in a personal and meaningful way. What's more, all of the content posted within a Community page (whether Public or Private to invited members) is indexed by Google search. Compared to posts on your Google+ page, Google+ Community updates should be a longer and more conversational, with more detail on a specific topic or a fuller explanation of the content you are sharing; something like you might see on a web message board, for example, complete with a question to finish in order to encourage feedback. To create a Community, simply select the Community tab on your Google+ page and click 'Create A Community'. Don't forget to tell your fans and customers that it exists, and encourage them to get involved.

In addition, search for Communities within your business sector or niche and actively participate in them to make connections, share expertise, and set yourself up as an authority figure. Once you are an established member of a Google+ Community, you begin to share content you have created regularly, to encourage more views and engagement with it. Carrying out this kind of self-promotion is *okay* when you are new to a Community, but you don't want to do it too often and risk coming over as spammy and unprofessional, which could eventually get you blocked from the Community altogether.

Got a physical presence? Use Google+ Local
If your business has a physical presence, make sure that you branch out onto the Google+ Local tab on your profile so that users will know that they can swing by and visit you.

If you don't already have a Google+ Local places page or want to claim one as yours, go to create a Google+ Page at https://plus.google.com/pages/create, select Local Business or Place as your business type, then enter your phone number. Google+ will connect you with your page if it already exists or prompt you to create one.

The benefits of Google+ Local pages
Google+ Local pages are indexed in Google search results, and display reviews, additional details and photos of a business beside it. As a result, a well-produced Local page that includes all of your most important business information has a good chance of getting high engagement with users.

Google+ Local users also receive prompts to review your business if they search for it on Google; all the influence of Local is compounded by Google becoming a more powerful resource for this type of interaction via its Google+ Local mobile app.

Connect with customers in Google+ Hangouts
Make use of the free video conferencing feature built into Google+ (Google+ Hangouts) to reach potential customers and professional connections. You can use Google+ Hangouts for all manner of purposes, from product demos to interviews, to live webinars (with screen-sharing), private meetings or pretty much anything else you can think of. Hangouts are a fantastic way to connect to your peers and extend your brand's reach, and particularly valuable if your business is not in a position to invest in expensive webinar or online meeting software. While you can only have 10 participants actively on video, you can stream the video to an unlimited number of viewers on YouTube using the Hangouts on Air feature, and the video is saved to your YouTube account for anyone to view at a later date.

As a way to grow your Hangouts On Air audience, submit your recordings to the directory at Hangouts on Air Shows (http://www.hoashows.com). HOAShows is one of the more regularly updated Hangouts On Air directories, and also a great place to find other great Hangouts On Air to join. Visit the Google+ Hangouts page at https://plus.google.com/hangouts to see what Hangouts are happening live right now.

Offer timely engagement

If someone likes or comments a post you make, be sure to reply to it as soon as possible. Any impact is all but lost if there is no reply within 24 hours. Notification Count is a Chrome extension that puts a counter right in your browser, next to the search bar, so you can always see how many new notifications you have. In addition, share a Google+ post easily on Facebook, LinkedIn or Twitter via the Chrome browser extension called Extend Share.

Check on Sparks

Sparks allows you to follow industry-related news; be sure to add your industry into Sparks to keep up to date with the latest in your field. The stories that you find can be re-distributed to your followers, cementing your page as a source of great information.

Test, measure and apply

As with all social media, the key to finding what strategy works best for your business on Google+ is to try experimenting with different types of posts and Hangouts and seeing what your followers engage most. Measure your performance via Google Analytics, as this is key to gaining more meaningful insights into your followers' behavior towards your activity. To focus specifically on the progress of custom campaigns and referral traffic, use Goals in Google Analytics in conjunction with giving links custom URLs via the Google URL Builder, found at http://bit.ly/googleurlbuildertool

Pinterest Tips:
Pin Your Way to Marketing Perfection

Pinterest allows anybody to create and organize virtual pinboards on almost any topic, then share these pins (which are most commonly images, but can also be in video form) to other Pinterest users and across the Internet via websites, blogs, and other social networks. Pins can either be uploaded directly from your computer or mobile device, or shared via a website. Since launching in March 2010, Pinterest's popularity has rocketed. When you consider that Pinterest is the second biggest driver of web traffic amongst social media sites (beaten only by Facebook), it is no surprise that thousands of businesses, including the biggest in the world, already use it as a place to showcase their brand to an audience of over 70 million users - over 75% of who browse the site on mobiles.

Pinterest users visit the site to browse and collate the things that they love and inspire them, and this is where the huge potential for businesses on Pinterest comes into play. The most successful pins on Pinterest - whether posted by an individual or a business - all have a couple of things in common: they pair super images with content that solves a problem, inspires a user, offers something desirable or appeals to a hobby or an activity. Think about how these pinnable traits can be applied to your area of brand as a way to drive engagement and click-through rates to your products, services, and content outside of Pinterest.

While *some* Pinterest users visit the site with the explicit desire to find a product to purchase, most do not, so the mix of content you provide should appeal to and positively influence both types. In short, if some of the mix of content you post makes someone want to buy from you, that's great, but if it makes them laugh, smile, or

95

daydream, that's a really good sign too. Pins that aren't solely promotional, but lifestyle-based and influential by positive association with your business can be just as effective in the long run. Whether your content offers a helpful tip or motivates a user to take an action, that's just more reason for them to repin it to one of their boards for safe keeping, and to show off to their followers via their Home screens.

No matter what your business, you should use Pinterest to inspire people with words and images. Show them their dreams and aspirations. This means creating boards not only to showcase your products and services, but others that demonstrate interesting and pinnable ideas, themes and concepts that surround it. For example, a coffee shop may have a board about their drinks and food, but also about the latest trends in coffee culture - gadgets, music, interior design, etc. People re-pin and follow accounts on Pinterest because they appeal to their passions and needs, not because they love your latest marketing campaign! Be a resource for pinners and pin with a service mindset, not one obsessed with profit.

Sign up as a business (or convert your personal Pinterest account)

In November 2012, Pinterest ramped up its support for brands by allowing them to sign up specifically as businesses (instead of just as an individual) and also allowed those brands which already had a Pinterest presence to convert their personal accounts to ones for business. To do either, visit http://business.pinterest.com, and select the option that applies to you. Once you're signed up as a business, you'll gain access to a selection of business-specific resources, including Pinterest analytics tools, successful case studies and links to Pinterest buttons and widgets you can place on your website or blog to promote your activity on the site.

Craft an effective username

The first thing you'll want to get right when signing up for Pinterest is your username, which will form the basis of your Pinterest profile's URL (e.g. www.pinterest.com/yourcompanyname). You will want to publicize this URL both online and in the real world, so try to keep it short, simple and memorable. The obvious choice is your brand name, but if you have a keyword or slogan related to your company that could work better (especially if your brand's name is longer than the 15-character limit), then consider that instead.

In addition, your 'First Name' and 'Last Name' should also reflect your brand, as it will appear prominently at the top of your Pinterest profile. My first and last names could be '500 Social Media' and 'Marketing Tips', for example. If your brand name is short, a last name may not be necessary.

Use the 'About' section to your advantage
The description you write in the About section of Pinterest appears at the top of your profile page, and acts to describe your brand and what you do. Crucially, however, it will also appear under your Pinterest URL in Google search results, so make sure to include two or three of your business' most relevant keywords. Don't overdo the length - 160 characters should be plenty. For example, mine reads: *"Andrew Macarthy, author of the #1 Amazon Web Marketing Bestseller, 500 Social Media Marketing Tips. Follow for social media tutorials and infographics!"*

Add your website and verify it for trustworthiness
Pretty obvious, this one. Pinterest will display a little 'globe' icon at the top of your profile, which will lead to your website when clicked. It isn't hugely prominent on the Pinterest profile page, but every little helps, so don't leave it blank. To show people that you are a trusted source of information, Pinterest allows you to verify your website. Once verified, you'll earn a tick next to its URL on

your profile and you'll also gain access to Pinterest web analytics. To verify your website on Pinterest, click the "Verify website" button next to the box in which you entered your URL. On the next page, follow the instructions to complete the verification process. You can verify using an HTML file or a meta tag.

Upload a great profile image

The importance of your Pinterest profile image cannot be overstated, as it is the visual representation of you and your brand across the whole of the site. The two most popular types of profile image for brands are your company's logo or, if you are the figurehead of your business, a head and shoulders shot - smiling and happy, of course. Ideally, your logo should be easily identified even at a small size, as this is how it will appear against your name when you like, comment, and re-pin content on Pinterest, and even smaller again when you appear in others' activity feeds. The ideal Pinterest profile image size is 180×180 pixels (or a larger image that scales exactly down to this size, as Pinterest will automatically do this when you upload it).

While most business users of Pinterest will prefer to use their company logo, there is also an argument for using a photo of a human face instead. Marketers often say that people like to do business with those they know, like and trust - and a person's face is naturally more trustworthy than a logo. In fact, many of the top pinners use images of themselves and not their company logo. Another option is to go for a hybrid approach - a head and shoulders snap with your company logo overlaid on top.

Install the 'Pin It' bookmarklet and add 'Pin It' buttons to your blog

The Pin It bookmarklet lets you grab an image or video from any website and pin it to one of your boards in an instant. Installing this ensures that you can quickly and easily pin top content to your boards as soon as you find it. When you visit a website and click 'Pin It' on a page where there is an image you want to pin (displayed in your browser's bookmarks bar), the bookmarklet will display thumbnails of all 'pinnable' images on that page. Simply select the one you want to share, choose the correct board, enter a description, and hit 'Pin It'.

Make sure that you install a Pinterest button on your blog, too (sit it beside the Facebook "Like" and "Tweet" buttons above, below, or to the side of each blog post. This strategy that ensures that your best images are made as easy for Pinterest users (who don't have the "Pin It" Bookmarklet at least) to share as possible.

Pinterest also has several choices of 'Follow' buttons, profile preview, and board preview widgets that you can display on your website to show off your Pinterest presence to potential fans. Choose the ones that take your fancy and embed them on your website where people will see them. There are simple step-by-step instructions for choosing and installing all of these widgets at the following address: http://pinterest.com/about/goodies/

Optimum Pinterest pin image sizes
Pinterest doesn't limit the vertical size of images pinned to its boards, but the horizontal width of pictures does max out at 735 pixels. Any image width will work, but it will be resized and displayed at a max of 735 pixels. Also keep this in mind: Pinterest only lets users pin from web pages where there is at least one image, and these images need to be a minimum size of 110 × 110 pixels big. So to encourage pinning from your own website and blog, be sure to add at least one pinnable image to every page or post.

Research shows taller images encourage more re-pins on Pinterest as they work better in the way the site stacks pieces of content on top of each another in its infinitely-scrolling, narrow-blocked grid. So if you want the images on your Pinterest account and blog to be shared more on Pinterest, focus on creating taller images. This isn't always possible, of course, but with image types such as infographics and step-by-step "how to" posts (both discussed below), there are several easy ways to implement this strategy into your Pinterest activity.

When and what to pin - be consistent and original
Pin regularly and consistently - a few times a day is a good target - but keep the stream going steadily, instead of weeks with nothing followed by huge bursts of activity. This strategy will maximize your exposure and prevent your followers from being flooded. Statistics reveal that around 80% of all content on Pinterest is made up of re-pinned pins, so aim to create original and inspiring pins to ensure that mean, more often than not, you are in that magic other 20%.

Keep your followers engaged by pinning content from a variety of sources, rather than just a couple of the same, over and over - i.e. not just stuff from your own website. And when you do pin content from others, build authority within your niche by sharing stuff that is inspirational, entertaining, accurate, up-to-date, helpful, and insightful. As a result, users of the site will come to think of your Pinterest boards as the destination to visit for reliable information about your business' main area of interest, and hopefully make many return visits!

Keep board names short and simple
In naming your boards, while you should be keyword-rich, keep the names simple and descriptive so that they can be found easily in Pinterest's search - but short enough so that the names do not trail off when viewed on your profile. Each of your board names can have up to 30 or so characters (including spaces) before being

cut off when viewed on your profile page - the remaining characters can be seen when the board is clicked on. In Pinterest search, meanwhile, the cut-off point is even shorter, at around 20 characters. If your board name is more than 20 characters long, try to put the most relevant keywords at the beginning so that you give it the best chance of being discovered.

When creating boards, keep "niche" in mind

If you have spent time on Pinterest, you might have noticed that some of the biggest brands on the site have created *loads* of pinboards; each very specific in its contents. While flooding your profile with pins might seem counter-intuitive from the "less is more" school of thought, in fact, it could pay dividends. Here's why: because people use Pinterest search a lot to find content (or come across it via a web search), creating highly targeted boards gives your pins a better chance of being found and viewed. For example, a board called "Wedding Inspiration" is very general - there are thousands all named the same and the chances of yours being found if you are just starting off as, say, a wedding accessories vendor, are slim. However, a board called "Pink Wedding Dresses 2014," although less likely to be searched for, has *much* less competition, and therefore gives it a better chance of being discovered in search results. So when you create your Pinterest boards, think unique, specific and niche, and target the content and keywords that you think your audience will be looking for.

Select an attractive board cover

One pin on each of your Pinterest boards will be used as the board cover. This image should be eye-catching, attractive and represent the board as a whole, on your profile and in search results. In short, your board cover should appeal to users enough to make them want to click and explore its contents in full. To select a pin as your board cover, hover over the board in question on your profile and click the 'Change Cover' button. Use the arrows to find the pin you want to use as your board cover. When selecting your board cover image, you can reposition the image to have the best part featured on the cover. Click Save Changes to apply the change.

Rearrange your Pinterest boards by importance
Pinterest gives you the option to rearrange your boards. All you need to do from your profile page is click, hold and drag boards into their optimum positions. The idea here is to shift your most important boards onto the first couple of rows - especially those 'above the fold', i.e. those boards visible onscreen before a user has to scroll down to see more. Think about which of your boards you want to feature most prominently - based on seasonal promotions, holidays, current trends, etc. and place them in the prime real estate areas of your Pinterest profile.

Create Secret Boards to collate pins and plan marketing
Pinterest's 'Secret Boards' feature allows you to create an unlimited number of hidden boards that can be made public at any time in the future. One simple and effective use for Secret Boards is related to seasonal campaigns, e.g. Valentine's Day, Thanksgiving, Christmas, etc. Slowly build up your campaign's themed Secret Board throughout the year and when the time comes, you'll be well prepared to make it public with a wealth of content which you can continue to add to during the promotional period. To create a Secret Board, choose the option at the bottom of your profile page; or, when creating a board from the 'Add' menu, make sure to switch the Secret Board slider to 'On'.

Drive repins and web traffic with effective pin descriptions and hashtags
Optimize the description of a pin by adding keywords and hashtags that users might use to find your product in Pinterest's

search. As Pinterest is one of the world's biggest drivers of traffic through to websites, my advice is to write descriptions as a useful and searchable piece of information, including keywords related to the pin and your business. Descriptions that mention how the subject of the pin provides value work better than straight explanations, so put yourself into the mind of a customer and write with what they might want to know in mind. For example, rather than saying something like *"We're now selling these diamond earrings, let us know what you think of them,"* a more effective description might read *"The way that the light bounces off these beautiful diamond earrings is mesmerizing, and they'd go well with any kind of outfit made for a night out on the town."*

Unlike other social networks where shorter copy is king, slightly longer descriptions work better on Pinterest; just enough to spark a user's curiosity so that they will feel compelled to click through to your website for more information. Oh, and just before you publish your pin, add a full URL back to the content within the description to boost its SEO. Always use the full URL, because Pinterest has a habit of marking shortened URLs (bit.ly, tinyurl, etc.) as spam. To encourage repinning (so that your pins are spread organically to a greater audience throughout the site), your description should also help people see the value of a pin and explain why they might want to repin it to one of their own boards.

As for hashtags, like with Twitter, don't go overboard - one or two are great; three is probably the maximum you want to consider before things start to look a bit spammy. Another good idea for your brand image and marketing (and something you can compound using other social networks and real-world efforts) is to create a hashtag specific to your brand, e.g. the name of your company or a short slogan (e.g. #mcdonalds or #imlovinit). Pepper this unique hashtag throughout your Pinterest activity and encourage your fans to do the same.

Modify blog image titles for optimum pinning from readers

The title you give an image when publishing it on your blog (that's the pop-up message you see when you hover your mouse cursor over it) is the text that Pinterest lifts to use as a pin's description when that image is pinned by a blog reader. So, if you encourage blog readers to pin content from your site, make sure that the image title (and subsequent pin description) appears as you would like it to when it lands on Pinterest. I often pin from websites where this hasn't been done, and if I'm not in the mood to optimize someone else's pin for them so that it doesn't look bad on my profile, then I'll just close the window and not bother. Don't let your readers do this to you!

Set up Rich Pins for greater visibility - especially for products

In May 2013, Pinterest began to roll out Rich Pins, a way to make pins more useful and engaging. With Rich Pins enabled, you'll be able to feature things like the price and availability of a product, recipe details, maps, etc. on top of and underneath relevant pins. Rich Pins update this information automatically and display it below a pin in real time by lifting data from your website.

Where Product Pins are concerned, the item in question will also be automatically added Pinterest's Gift category feed (http://www.pinterest.com/gifts/). Pinterest's own research shows that Product Pins get higher click-through rates than regular pins and make your brand more visible on the site. What's more, users will receive an email notification if Product Pins they've saved drop in price, encouraging them to buy right there, particularly if they weren't quite ready to at the higher price.

To get started with Rich Pins, you'll need to prep your website with meta tags, test out the function and apply to get them on Pinterest. Getting Rich Pins to work right requires some coding and technical knowhow, so if you're unsure what terms like "oEmbed" and "semantic markup" mean, I recommend getting together with your web developer for a chat and pointing him or her to http://business.pinterest.com/rich-pins/ for more info. Once you overcome the slight technical hurdle, there are plenty of reasons to use Rich Pins including the likelihood of increased likes, repins, web traffic, and sales - definitely worth the effort!

Pin more to your most popular boards
After you have been using Pinterest for a while, naturally you will begin to notice that some of your boards are more popular than others. Keep an eye on the boards that have gained the most followers and, while not neglecting your other boards (you want to continue to build and cater to their audiences too), give a little extra attention to your most-followed boards, i.e. post to them a bit more frequently, in order to reach the largest number of people that you can and to help increase the number of re-pins and followers you earn.

Get inspired with consumer insight
Pinterest users' boards reveal a lot about their likes, interests, wishes and desires. Use this to your advantage, by snooping at your followers' boards and tailoring your business' product range and Pinterest content to suit. In addition, click on the "Popular" link from the drop-down menu on the Pinterest home page to research what's hot with Pinterest users right now, then work out if it is suitable for you to integrate these trends into your content strategy.

Use quality images and videos
Photos and videos are central to Pinterest, so make sure yours are good quality and that they can be pinned (non-flash) and are tagged correctly. Pinterest supports videos from YouTube and Vimeo. Share images that people can relate and respond to. That way you'll increase the likelihood that they'll find value in what you

have to show and are more likely to engage and interact. Draw attention to your site's videos by using annotations that ask users to "pin this video to Pinterest". Once pinned, they go into Pinterest's dedicated video section.

Overlay text on your images to grab attention and encourage interaction

Most Pinterest users scan the site's content and don't take the time to read the descriptions or comments associated with an image - that is unless the image grabs their attention first! Images overlaid with easy-to-read, bold text do that particularly well in drawing people's attention, clarifying the message of the pin, and encouraging interaction. Use free services such as Pinwords (http://www.pinwords.com/) to achieve this result easily and stylishly.

Create a video board

Pinned videos from sites including YouTube and Vimeo will play directly within Pinterest (i.e. no need to click through to view). If videos are part of your marketing strategy, make sure your customers know about them via Pinterest. For example, I have separate video boards that showcase my social media marketing tutorials for Facebook, Twitter, Pinterest, and others.

One of the downsides of posting a video to Pinterest is that the pin itself - a randomly chosen video still - does not often have the same visual impact as a specially chosen image, and therefore will not encourage viewers to engage as much with the content. To help overcome this, make use of YouTube and Vimeo's custom thumbnail features. The thumbnail you choose will act as the image that represents your video pin, so make it interesting!

Experiment with animated GIFs on Pinterest

While the popularity of animated GIFs has never been disputed, in recent years their usage online has boomed thanks to more accessible creation tools, faster Internet connections, and the speed and ease at which they can be digested by viewers. Animated GIFs were rolled out to Pinterest in January 2014 and they are an easy way for brands to add a fun, engaging element to their boards. A few methods for their use include: demonstrating a tricky step in a how-to guide, replaying a hilarious moment from a recent event or ad campaign, flashing up the benefits of a product or service, or simply relaying an emotion like happiness, surprise, or fear. Mix up images, videos, and animated GIFs to see which best resonate with your audience.

To ensure that you and your team have access to your database of GIFs at any time, consider setting up a free Tumblr account on which to upload and store them. The micro-blogging site is synonymous with GIFs, and allows you to create password-protected blogs, and a way to grant access to multiple users.

Observe, comment, and reply
Pinterest allows you to mention other users in a comment by typing @username. People love knowing you like their content, so be sure to let them know. Create a seed-list of loyal people you can count on to re-pin your content, and @tag them in your pins to get them involved.

Encourage interaction, add another pinner
Pinterest is all about sharing, so encourage selective, loyal followers to pin to your boards, being sure to allow your most trusted brand ambassadors to pin with you when you create a new board. Just enter their username in the 'Add another pinner' box. Use the viral nature of Pinterest to your advantage too.

Encourage comments and ask for likes

Use your new pins and boards as opportunities to interact with other users to gain likes, comments and re-pins. Create interest in your own content by asking users to let you know what they think, asking them to 'like' if they're impressed, or to guess where a particular photo was taken. With so much pinning to do, don't forget that engaging with other users should be your top priority - like, comment and re-pin just as much as you encourage others; it'll benefit you in the long run.

See who's sharing your content

Want to see who and what content Pinterest users are grabbing from your website? Use the URL http://pinterest.com/source/*[yourpinterestusername]* to see what's been shared from your website or blog. You can then use this information to see what types of content is most popular with your follow base, and go on to optimize your output as a result.

Pinterest Board Ideas for Business

Create a VIP board to feature customers

Ask fans of your brand to pin pictures of themselves with their favorite product of yours, and to tag you in the description. You can re-pin those photos onto a VIP board on your profile. Not only is this a great way to play to the 'vanity' of your fans (they love to be featured on your boards), but it also serves to spread the word of your brand around the social network.

Create a products and services board, give sneak peeks

While you should never use Pinterest as a way to spam your customers with marketing pins, a couple of boards dedicated to your products and services won't harm, particularly as Pinterest is such a *huge* driver of sales and web traffic. Fashion brands on Pinterest are experts at this strategy, posting new boards to reflect the changing season's must-have looks and provide exclusive sneak peeks to its fans. A study by Vision Critical for the clothing brand J. Crew found that nearly a quarter (21%) of Pinterest users visited the store to buy an item they liked or pinned from its boards. The same survey revealed that a whopping 80% tended to buy an item within three weeks of pinning it. To boost this statistic even further, J. Crew tempts customers with pin descriptions like *"Love what you see? Our Very Personal Stylist team can help you pre-order this look before it becomes available on Wednesday August 21.) Call or email..."*

Create a current campaigns board
Build a board specifically for posting information about your latest marketing campaigns, offers and deals, so that your customers can find them all in one place, e.g. Summer Offers, 25% Off Sale, etc. Make sure that you rearrange your boards to make this one appear near the top of your profile, so that these limited-time deals are given as much visibility as possible.

Create a meet-the-team board
Pinterest pins provide the perfect opportunity for your customers to get to know you and your staff better. Take individual photos of your employees and use the title and description to tell your customers who they are and what they do; add other interesting snippets of information, e.g. their hobbies, favorite movie or why they love working for you! In essence, take customers behind the scenes, to help them connect more closely with you and your brand.

Create a company history board
Take inspiration from Facebook's Milestones feature and use pins to document the history of your business. Customers love to indulge in the history and heritage of their favorite brands, and Pinterest provides the perfect opportunity to let them do this.

Showing that your company has a history improves your credibility; showing your growth and new products can imply core growth, stability and trustworthiness. Examples of stuff you can feature as part of your history include storefront or website changes, product package revisions through the years - and even pictures of you in your younger days!

Utilize Place Pins Boards

In November 2013, Pinterest rolled Place Pins – a way for users to geotag their activity on the site. Place Pin boards allow users to see exactly where the subject of a Pin was snapped or created, and also include extra information like an address and phone number so that anyone can easily find you, and even get directions. To create a Place Pin board, select "Add a map" when you create a new board, or edit an existing board's settings to add one. Then, click on each pin individually to search for a location and add it to the board's map.

Place Pins have numerous uses that include: marking bricks and mortar locations or an upcoming event, showing off where your clients are around the country or world (to impress with your geographical influence), to pin ideas for your customers based on location (e.g. showing how your product or service adapts to or is used in different places), or as part of a contest (e.g. ask customers to pin photos of themselves using their product or service wherever they are in the world, and offer a prize to the one that is the most imaginative, beautifully shot, farthest away, etc.).

Showcase your blog and website

Create a board specifically to pin blog posts and articles that you have created on your website - it helps to drive traffic to your content. Also use these boards to highlight and re-purpose old (but still great) blog posts that were posted before the invention of Pinterest.

Create and share infographics

Infographics are a hugely popular way to share information on the web, and they look fantastic in Pinterest's vertical layout. Consider creating your own infographics to share with customers (don't forget to plug your business at the bottom of them). Also repin the best infographics you find on Pinterest or around the web, as long as they are relevant and interesting to your audience. I created a Pinterest board dedicated to social media infographics and its content is amongst my most viewed and re-pinned.

Create a tutorials and 'how-to' board

In such a creative space as Pinterest, putting together tutorials and how-to videos related to your business or industry works really well. In a step-by-step process, use one pinned picture, GIF, or video per step to create an easy-to-follow chain of instructions and increase your exposure at the same time. Alternatively (and given the evidence that taller images get more re-pins), create a single tall image made up of several smaller step-by-step photos and instructions.

Create a reviews and recommendations board

A great number of people use Pinterest to get shopping inspiration, and associate themselves with brands and retailers. Write up reviews and recommendations for products that people want and pin them to a board with a title such as 'Products We Love', whether the items inside are yours or not. Even if they aren't yours - good karma reciprocates good karma on Pinterest, and you'll see a long-term positive trend if you feature and tag others in this kind of way.

Hold a Pinterest contest

Like other social media outlets, Pinterest is a great way to hold contests to increase engagement and loyalty. The easier your contest is to enter, the simpler it is to setup and the more entries you are likely to receive. Examples include asking entrants to pin images from your business website to enter, asking fans to upload original images of their favorite products from your brand, or asking them to pin creations they have made by using one of your products (for example, a sausage company could ask participants to pin images and recipes of meals they have concocted in the kitchen). For a full rundown on the Dos and Don'ts of Pinterest contests and how to comply with its terms of service, visit this page: http://business.pinterest.com/logos-and-marketing-guidelines/

Run an offer on Pinterest
People love offers - anything with the word 'free', 'discount' or 'giveaway' in it - and the visual nature of Pinterest is a great way to get them noticed. Either pin images from your website and add a description of the offer featured there, or upload a pin direct to the site for an 'exclusive to Pinterest followers' offer. And how about getting even fancier, with something like a 'pin it to unlock' campaign? Upload a pin detailing a special offer and tell your followers it will only run once the image has been re-pinned 'X' number of times, encouraging them to like, comment, and re-pin to unlock it!

Use Facebook to promote your Pinterest content
On your Facebook fan page, show images of your favorite pins to your fans. Provide a mixture of links, fun status updates and your specific boards. Be sure to include the URL to the pins in question, so that Facebook fans are encouraged to click through to view, re-pin and follow. One of the most effective ways I use this technique is with infographics. For example, let's assume the pinned infographic is called '10 Ways to Delight Your Blog Readers'. I will copy the image into a photo editor and crop it to show only the first of the ten ways. I'll then upload and post this shortened image

to Facebook, along with a post that describes the infographic and tells fans to click through to Pinterest, at the link provided, if they want to see the other nine points.

LinkedIn Tips:
Network Like Clockwork

LinkedIn is the web's central hub for professionals and businesses to connect and market their brand, expertise, and skills to the world. With powerful networking tools and company profiles, it is a great resource to help build your business, both through your personal profile and Company Page.

As an individual on LinkedIn, you can - among other things - use the site to establish a professional profile and control one of the top search results for your name, build a broad network of professional connections whose knowledge you can tap into, and discover new business opportunities.

A LinkedIn Company Page is a place for companies to provide more information about themselves, their products and services, job opportunities, and where they can share expert insights. Any LinkedIn user can follow a company that has set up a Company Page to receive and interact with updates on their home page, which allows you a chance to drive awareness of you and your brand.

Research by LinkedIn revealed that you only need 100-200 followers of your Company Page to reach the tipping point to start making an impact and driving engagement, so it's well worth making sure both it and your personal profile is doing the best job it can. Use these tips to make that possible:

Note: Many of this chapter's tips are prefixed with either "Personal Profile" or "Company Pages," and some with both. This will help you tell where the advice given is best applied. Where there is no prefix, the tip is a more general hint about one of LinkedIn's many features.

Personal Profile and Company Page: Fill them in completely
Make sure you fill out all of the sections on your LinkedIn profiles, and that you set up both a personal LinkedIn profile for you individually, and one that is specifically for your business - a LinkedIn Company Page. Either page might be the first port of call for a potential client, so you'll want to make a good first impression.

Important personal profile sections
The Description section is one of the most important of your personal LinkedIn profile, as you can really expand upon your current and past roles and responsibilities, and your achievements. It's also a really good place for you to drop in some relevant keywords, which will aid your chances of appearing higher in LinkedIn's search.

With a quick glance at your personal profile, visitors will know what you've done at each of your jobs, can learn more about you and determine whether you're someone they want to connect with to foster a new professional relationship.

To make a prospect's job even easier, use short paragraphs or bullet-pointed lists. If you use bullets, start your sentences with verbs (past tense verbs for past positions, present tense verbs for present positions). Rather than state what you did, tell people what you accomplished or how you helped the business progress. The more concrete and quantifiable you can be here, the better.

The Summary section as is also crucial, as it is your first opportunity to write an overview or statement about who you are and what you can offer your audience, and a chance to show what makes you unique and desirable to prospective connections. Make sure your Summary expresses who you are *as a person*. Your company website or LinkedIn Company Page is there to tell people about your company, but your personal profile is there for LinkedIn users to learn more about you!

How to Create A Company Page

To add a Company Page, sign in to LinkedIn as a personal user and click on the "Companies" link in the bar at the top of the site. From here, click the 'Add A Company' button, which is positioned at the top of the page on the right-hand side. There are a few small milestones you have to reach, and a few simple administrative technicalities to overcome before LinkedIn will allow you to get started, but it won't take you long before you're ready to rock.

Note: You must have a company email address, e.g. yourname@yourcompany.com, in order to create a LinkedIn Company Page. You are not permitted to use an address with a domain such as Outlook or Gmail.

Once your Company Page is created, you can begin to flesh it out with details about your location, size, contact details, industry, etc. by clicking Edit at the top-right hand corner of your company's Home tab.

Important Company Page sections

Obviously, the 'Company Description' section is very important. Write a high-level overview of your business that showcases your brand and tells people what makes you unique. It is the perfect place to start spreading your message and opening up avenues of conversation with potential partners.

The 'Specialties' section of your Company Page overview is also very powerful. Here, enter relevant keywords about who you are and what you do, so that there is a greater chance that you'll be found more often in a LinkedIn search.

Create Showcase Pages for specific products or services
In November 2013, LinkedIn introduced Showcase Pages, a dynamic replacement for the old Company Page "Product and Services" tabs, which were removed from the site in April 2014. Showcase Pages aren't the same as Company Pages, and they don't have all of the same features. Think of Showcase Pages as children to the parent Company Page: a way to extend your LinkedIn presence by posting regular updates about a *specific* product, service, department, business initiative, etc. rather than your business as a whole, and a place where you can share unique and specific aspects of your brand to a more concentrated and distinct audience. For example, Microsoft has a main Company Page, but several Showcase Pages for products and services Office and Microsoft Training and Certification.

Users can follow and receive updates from Showcase Pages in the same way as any Company Page, so keep the top-notch content flowing with images, links, videos, freebies, etc. If an update appeals to both your wider fan base via your main Company Page *and* the more niche audience of a Showcase Page, don't be afraid to re-purpose it. Showcase Pages have their own unique URL for easy sharing, and also feature on the right-hand side of your Company Page. After identifying an area (or areas - you can create up to 10 Showcase Pages) of your business for which a Showcase Page would be useful, here's how you create one:

How to create a Showcase Page:
1. Click the down arrow next to the blue Edit button on the Company Page, and select "Create a Showcase Page."
2. Enter the new Page's name and assign administrators.
3. Click Create.

117

Optimum Showcase Page branding image sizes:
Hero (cover) image: Minimum 974 x 330 pixels.
Logo: 100 x 60 pixels.
Square logo: 50 x 50 pixels.

To make creating your desired Showcase Page cover photo as easy as possible, I have built a free template for use with Adobe Photoshop or GIMP. Once you have downloaded the template (which is in a .psd format), follow the instructions within it to insert your design, then save the file as a .png ready for upload to LinkedIn. Grab your free template via the link in the *Free Social Media Templates chapter of this book.*

Personal Profile and Company Pages: add a profile photo, logo and banner images
On your personal profile, add a recent photo to humanize it - quite a few people don't, to their own detriment. LinkedIn profile pics are 200×200 pixels in size. Keep it smart, though - don't post a photo on your LinkedIn profile of you in your bathing suit on the beach - a head and shoulders shot of you looking smart and presentable is best. And as with your profile information, keep your profile photo updated with your changing look - hairstyles, glasses, wardrobe, etc. This will ensure that you are recognizable at meetings, conferences and events at which you and your LinkedIn connections attend!

The default landing tab for your Company Page on LinkedIn is the Home tab, and this is where your company logo and banner image will appear. It's very similar to how your Facebook cover image looks, but the size is different. The optimum size for a LinkedIn cover image is 646×222 pixels; the profile photo remains a square, but this time it is shrunk to 50×50 pixels. Use this space to illustrate and extend your unique branding message. Banner images can also be added to the Products and Careers tabs.

How to upload a logo or banner image
1. Click Edit at the top of your Company Page homepage.
2. Locate the Image or Logo section and click the Add image link or Edit (whichever is present).
3. Click Upload to attach your image file, and then click Save.
4. Click Publish in the top right of the page.

Personal Profile: re-order job positions by importance
LinkedIn will automatically order your job positions in chronological order, but you can override this and arrange them by importance to you (and potential connections) by clicking on the up and down arrow icon next to any position and then dragging and dropping it into whatever order you like.

Personal Profile: craft a catchy headline
Your personal LinkedIn profile headline is the first piece of information a potential connection will see about you, so make it catchy and individual. Something generic like "Retail Manager" is not enough - there are millions of those on LinkedIn. Think about what differentiates you, what makes you special and what you want to be known for. Craft a headline to match. At the time of writing, my headline reads: Andrew Macarthy - Social Media Consultant, Bestselling Social Media Author, Content Curator.

Another quick trick is to update your personal profile headline every couple of months, which seems to help boost views within search, and ensures your profile's keywords will be found by different people typing different search terms.

Note: If you're feeling sneaky, you can also add your email address in your headline so that people can contact you directly, without having to go through LinkedIn, which often won't let you e-mail someone without having connected first - although this *can* look a little unprofessional.

The more people who view your profile, the more likely a percentage of those visitors will click through to your (or your company's) website or blog to learn more about you and maybe encourage them to connect. In summary, lure prospects in with a thoroughly filled out headline and page, and win them with your expertise.

Personal Profile: Grab a vanity URL
When you edit your LinkedIn profile, go to the "public profile" section to create your LinkedIn URL of choice. As with other social networks, this will make directing potential clients to a memorable address that much easier.

Personal Profile: Optimize your location
Entering your location on LinkedIn might not be *quite* as obvious as it first seems. For example, I have spent a lot of time in Berwyn, IL, a city that is just a stone's throw from the much bigger and better-known Chicago - so let's pretend for a moment that I live in Berwyn. If a prospect scouring LinkedIn was in charge of finding people from the Chicagoland area, listing my location as Chicago will help me appear in more search results (if filtered by location), and I will also be seen as someone "local" to others within my target market. Think about how this tactic might apply to your location and adjust your profile accordingly.

Personal Profile: showcase your Achievements
LinkedIn allows users to add projects, languages, publications, awards, test scores, courses, patents, certifications and volunteering carried out to your profile. As you can imagine if you put yourself in the shoes of a potential connection, this will add a lot of value to

your profile, both in business terms and showing you off as a well-rounded individual. So if you have these details to add, make sure you do so.

Personal Profile: utilize applications
Connect applications of interest to your profile. Applications such as Slideshare and Amazon Reading List give others insights into your interests and professional activities.

Personal Profile: promote your company through employee profiles
Getting all employees on board with your LinkedIn strategy is crucial to its success, as it helps to create an extended network that amplifies your company's standing and influence on the site. Ask your employees to create their own LinkedIn accounts and to list your company as their employer. If necessary, provide them with training on how to build a great LinkedIn Profile (shameless plug: check out my book, *How to Build the Ultimate LinkedIn Profile in Under an Hour*, for a step-by-step guide), and pass on the benefits that growing their own professional network can provide.

Rather than being scared that employee profiles will make them a target for headhunters from rival firms, see them as reflecting extremely well on your business instead. It is likely that many of your employees already have LinkedIn accounts and, sadly, there isn't much you can do to stop them moving on if they decide to - just focus on the positives.

Personal Profile: follow other companies
Company follows make it possible for you to keep your eye on key events happening at companies you're interested in, handy for keeping tabs on the opposition and for your own inspiration. You can follow or stop following a company from its Company Page.

To follow a company:

1.   Click Companies at the top of your homepage.

2.   Search for a company.

3.   Click Follow in the upper right of the company's Home page.

To stop following a company:

1.   Click Profile at the top of your homepage and scroll down to the Following box on your profile.

2.   In the Companies section, move your cursor over the grey Following link underneath the company's name.

3.   Click on Unfollow.

Personal Profile: Use Advanced Search and Get Introduced to find prospects and earn trust that leads to sales/partnerships. LinkedIn's Advanced search function is a great way to find potential new prospects. You can filter by relationship, groups, industry, and location, then even save the search for use in future. Even if you can't connect with someone directly, you might be able to pick up enough clues to contact them outside of LinkedIn, via their website or other social profile. *Or,* make use of the Get Introduced feature. This allows you to contact members of LinkedIn who are in our 2nd degree or 3rd degree network. Here's how:

1. On the profile of the person you want to connect to, click "Get introduced through a connection" on the right-hand side of the profile. If only one of you can make the introduction, the Request an Introduction page will appear.

2. Hover your mouse pointer over the arrow next to the Send InMail button and click Get introduced. If more than one person can make the introduction, you may choose who you want to make the introduction.

3. Write and send your message.

In the same way you are thoughtful and gracious to people who want to connect with you, do the same when you want to connect to others - do not be salesy! Greet them by name and add a short note that personalizes your invitation, e.g. genuine evidence that you have enjoyed a blog post they wrote or a lecture they gave in which you were attendance. Complete your invitation by offering a compelling reason why you should connect with one another. These extra touches can help to flatter a potential connection, make a good first impression, and increase your chances of developing a relationship.

Once you have successfully connected with a prospect, do your best to help the relationship blossom. Depending on the reasons you connected in the first place, and your overall goals, your follow-up strategy will differ. It could be as simple as setting up a reminder using the LinkedIn Contacts feature to "touch base" over the course of several weeks, or to sweeten things up by offering a free quote, PDF, or other valuable resource out of the goodness of your heart. When the relationship is sufficiently strong, you can think about moving the conversation offline as a way to get things moving towards your end goal, e.g. providing a product or service, or striking up a meaningful partnership.

Personal Profile: Accept quality, relevant invites

As well as looking to connect with others, start accepting invitations from those who want to connect with you. The more connections you have, the larger your expanded network grows, in turn creating more opportunities down the line. Unfortunately, spammers are present on LinkedIn as they are on all social networks, so be careful only to accept invites from reputable and relevant profiles.

Personal Profile: use tags and notes to efficiently organize connections

LinkedIn's Contacts feature (accessed via the Networks menu at the top of site) lists all of your connections on the social network. One of its most useful functions is the ability to tag individual people with custom labels. Doing so will allow you to group and organize different types of individuals (hot prospects, existing clients, thought leaders, etc.), so that you can sort, find, and contact them as quickly as efficiently as possible whenever the need arises. Just click 'tag' below a contact, then choose from the existing suggestions, or invent your own. Once done, you can filter connections by tag from the menu at the top of the Contacts page.

Taking organization and efficiency a step further, when you click on a contact to view their full profile, you will see a "Relationship" tab near the top, marked by a star. Click this to reveal several options, including a space to type notes about that person, add how you met, and a function to set reminders about them, e.g. when you need to follow-up with them. All of the information in this section is only visible to you.

Note: Your Contacts page will also alert you to significant events in the professional lives of your connections, such as when they start a new job. Be sure to send a quick note to acknowledge a contact's success, keep in touch, and continue to reinforce your bond.

Personal Profile: recommend and endorse others

The more you give on LinkedIn, the more you'll get back later on down the line. Recommend and endorse others often - especially colleagues and even competitors - even if they don't ask you first. Each time you give or receive an endorsement, it will appear in the LinkedIn news feed for your network, which means more visibility for you and your brand. As you'll discover, endorsing somebody almost always results in them returning the favor, and as your endorsements grow you may even want to move that section towards the top of your profile to showcase your most valuable skills to potential contacts. Do keep in mind that you want your endorsements to be received as genuine and well deserved (more so by other users than the recipient, in a lot of cases), so don't go overboard on your first round of endorsements for an individual; spread your efforts out so that it doesn't come across as spammy or a suspicious act of over-praising.

A good rule of thumb is to review each invitation request received and make sure that the person in question has at least completed their profile and added a photo. Also ensure that the connection is purposeful and relevant to you and your brand. Do they, in your head, offer a good reason to connect, or do they personally tell you why they want to? Do you know them already, or have they worked in the same industry as you? Lastly, always reply when accepting a genuine and interesting connection request. This is an easy way to start forming relationships.

Personal Profile and Company Pages: write compelling, descriptive content

Most LinkedIn profiles are snorefests from start to finish. Add some personality with humor, and perhaps an interesting story in your summary. At the very least, tell visitors who you are, what you do, who you help and how you can help them, so there is some direction for people when they land on your profile. While you want your profile's tone to be engaging, do keep things professional to reflect the more formal environment that LinkedIn maintains compared to other social networks.

Personal Profile and Company Pages: insert bullet points to make your pages more readable

If you've filled out your LinkedIn profile in full, you've probably got quite a lot of text on there, some of which (achievements, responsibilities, etc.) would be *so* much easier for prospects to read in a bulleted list. As it happens, you *can* insert bullet points into your LinkedIn profile sections, but it's not something LinkedIn shouts about. Here's how:

1. Sign into LinkedIn and click "Edit Profile" at the top of your profile page.
2. Scroll to the section of the profile where you want to add bullet points and click the pencil icon.
3. Place your cursor at the beginning of the line where you want to add a bullet point, and type "•" (without the speech marks). Do this for as many lines as you wish, then click Save.
4. You're done, and your text should be bulleted. If you ever return to edit a section that you have added bullets to, the "•" code will not be visible; it is replaced with a single space at the beginning of a line. To remove the bullet, delete this space and click Save.

Personal Profile and Company Pages: Write for LinkedIn SEO, use relevant keywords

When you optimize your LinkedIn pages with relevant keywords to you, your expertise and your business, it stands a chance of ranking higher in Google and LinkedIn search. Don't make it too obvious by writing in an unnatural style that renders it blatant to readers that you are trying to crunch in as many keywords as possible - but be aware that you'll want to include them nonetheless. Whenever you gain new skills and expertise, don't forget to add these into your profile too. LinkedIn allows you to add up to 50 skills, so fill in as many as you can.

The keywords you use should be a mix - from broad terms to those that are very specific, as you never know which search terms someone will be using to potentially find you. Where you put these keywords matters, too - research by blogging4jobs.com revealed that your name, headline, company name, job title, and skills keywords rank the highest.

Another important place to use keywords on your personal LinkedIn profile is in the job experience section, both for your current and past positions. Use lots of detail, going into the same amount of depth that you would on your resume about the role you did, the responsibilities you had and the goals you achieved. Don't be afraid to brag a bit!

Personal Profile, Showcase, and Company Pages: link to your LinkedIn profiles in emails and on your website
Be sure to include your LinkedIn personal profile URL in your email signature, on your website, info tab on your Facebook profile and blog, as well as on your printed marketing collateral and business cards.

You can also attract new followers and boost engagement by adding your LinkedIn Company Page product reviews to your website. Adding product reviews in this way provides real credibility for potential customers, and can help to boost conversion rates.

On landing pages or those on which you want to boost conversion, test *long* as opposed to *short* product recommendations. You may also want to experiment with different types of recommendations based on the visitor coming to your page, e.g. first time as opposed to regular visitor.

Personal Profile, Showcase, and Company Pages: drive traffic with value-added updates and an emphasis on images
Like other social media sites, focus on providing interesting and value-added updates to help others succeed in business. Research

shows that the types of updates that resonate most with LinkedIn users are the sharing of expertise and industry insights, but of course you may want to talk about company developments and new products from time to time, too. The updates you share on your Company Page are displayed prominently on the main Home tab and include a nice big space for images, so don't forget to make them compelling too; for personal accounts, updates appear in a feed visible when users sign in.

When you post an update to LinkedIn, you will need to copy and paste your link to the specific article and LinkedIn will automatically pull in the image and post for you. From there you can edit and publish your update. Use questions or ask for feedback to drive engagement! Remember that you can delete the URL that you pasted into the update after LinkedIn has found the website in question. This will keep your update looking more clean, concise, and clickable.

Personal Profile: mention LinkedIn users and companies in updates to heighten engagement
In April 2013, LinkedIn introduced mentions to its social network, allowing you to easily and effectively tag connections and companies in your updates, as well as in comments. LinkedIn mentions also seamlessly integrate with Twitter handles. When a person or company is mentioned, they will be notified within their LinkedIn profile. Here's how to start:

1.   Begin by typing the name of a connection or a company in your LinkedIn status update box or a comment field on the Homepage.
2.   Select someone from the list of your connections that appear in the drop-down, complete your status or comment and post it.

By mentioning individuals and companies in your updates, your ability to engage and grow connections with business partners and customers is given a welcome boost.

Personal Profile, Showcase, and Company Pages: be visible, valuable and timely

When you've built up a thriving network of connections, you're going to want to maintain that reputation. To do this, remain consistently visible, valuable and timely in your participation in all areas of LinkedIn. Your most recent activity will appear near the top of your profile, but if you're not very active, nothing will show. As with other social networks, a rate of activity that works out at about one or two updates a day is a good target to aim for.

If you need some inspiration as to what to share with your network, check out LinkedIn Today for trending news topics, as well as the LinkedIn INfluencer program to share and comment on insights from well-known individuals across a variety of business sectors.

Use the Notifications option at the top of your profile to review the most recent interactions from your network, and respond in a timely manner. To keep on top of what might be a myriad of updates and choose what you want to get involved with, filter the updates on your LinkedIn homepage by Shares to see, at a glance, what is trending on your network.

Personal Profile, Company Pages, and Showcase Pages: add images, files, questions, links and contests to company status updates

LinkedIn allows companies to add images and files to their status updates, so you definitely want to experiment with these to help attract eyeballs onto your posts and encourage engagement - whether that be someone clicking on a link to your blog posts, commenting, entering a contest or anything else. The number of likes and comments a post gets can signal high engagement, but the click-through data can provide even more insight into what your audience is really attracted to.

Contests are a cheap and easy option, and a great way of attracting new leads on LinkedIn. These can be as simple as offering your followers the chance to win a gift card, product or free consultation for everyone who 'likes' your status over the course of a week. Pick a random winner and use their happiness and the interaction between you to cultivate more posts and spread positivity about your brand to new and existing customers.

Personal Profile, Company Pages, and Showcase Pages: update regularly

Be sure to update your LinkedIn profile and Company page periodically to make sure that all of the information is up to date. Every time you update your personal profile or post a status from your Company page, the change is shared to your network and followers. The more people who view your profile, the more likely a percentage of those visitors will click through to your (or your company's) website or blog to learn more about you and maybe encourage them to connect. In summary, lure prospects in with thoroughly filled-in pages, and win them with your expertise.

Personal Profile: Publish original "thought leader" content and grow a tribe of followers

Previously limited to an elite group of people, LinkedIn opened up its publishing platform to all users in February 2014. It allows you to post full blogs on LinkedIn that become part of your professional profile, and they are also sent out to your network as a status update. Ideally, you want to use the publishing platform as a way to share value-driven (non-salesy), expert content to both your current and potential audience. Potential topics include important trends in your industry, what advice you would give to someone hoping to enter your field of work, the biggest challenges your industry needs to solve, etc. There is no word limit, but some of the best examples so far aren't "full-on blog replacement" in length either. If you are inspired to come up with something between 400 and 600 words once a week that will build your credibility and strengthen your standing on the site, that is just what LinkedIn is looking for.

To start writing, click on the pencil icon in the usual status update box, and a familiar word processing layout (complete with the options to add links, videos, and images) will appear. Once you've finished writing, conclude your post with a call to action if necessary, but definitely include a quick few lines of bio with links back to your LinkedIn profile, website, or blog. When the post is shared to LinkedIn, re-post it on your Company page and other social networks for maximum exposure, then keep an eye on the metrics LinkedIn provides to help determine how well your content is resonating with your audience. As you publish more and the breadth of your statistics grows, you will be able to replicate the kind of post that does well.

Note: LinkedIn is rolling this feature out to everyone over the course of a few months, so if you can't take advantage yet, it shouldn't be too long until you can.

Personal Profile: join and analyze targeted Groups
This is a biggie. Whatever your industry, get involved in niche Groups related to your industry as a way to connect with others, discuss and learn new ideas, and - more subtly - as a way to connect with key partners and find out what your target market is interested in. Use the ideas you find over time - from popular discussions, statuses with the most likes and comments, etc. - to help you work on ideas and topics to feature in your company's

status updates. To help you discover new LinkedIn Groups, select Interests" from the menu at the top of your LinkedIn homepage, then click "Groups." You can also use this landing page to manage all future group participation.

As you're looking for groups to join (one or two that you can dedicate yourself to rather than loads that you can't is better, by the way), don't just evaluate the discussions taking place, but also the Top Contributors panel for people you might want to connect with. If you are already in a group, securing a spot in the Top Contributors box can be a way to showcase yourself as an authority figure in your business sector and attract others to you through "follows" and potential opportunities to connect. Regular positive interaction, like posting and commenting thoughtful topics and responses will raise your standing in the group, while promotional, spam, negative or inappropriate content will damage it.

If a group you intend to join is already well established, you can easily view and search for popular topics within it to see what type of questions and issues are drawing the most engagement and whether these are of interest to you and your business. Most easy is to simply click the "Popular" tab at the top of the group for a general overview. For a more thorough search:

1. Visit a group where your target market is active and click on the Search tab. Notice a box on the left-hand side which allows you can search for posts by post type.
2. Use the search function to find the most engaging content on a given topic.
3. Create a log of the types of topics, questions and challenges which are being discussed by your target market.

Start your own LinkedIn Group

If you can't find a Group that's right for you, launching and developing a LinkedIn Group can have many benefits for businesses, including:

Building more awareness about you within your target markets
Positioning your company (or you as an individual) as an industry thought leader
Nurturing valuable industry relationships
A showcase for your great industry-leading content and products
Generation of interest and inquiries for your business
Converting Group members to subscribers and advocates for your brand
A place to test status updates and see what engagement they receive, before adding them to your company stream.

LinkedIn Group title and description
The right LinkedIn Group name is critical to attracting the right members, so include plenty of relevant keywords in the title and description, as this is what will appear both in a LinkedIn search and indexed by Google. Thinking more about the description, use words and phrases that will encourage people to join and differentiate you from the competition.

Around 48 characters and 140 characters will appear in search results for your Group title and description respectively, so make them count!

Draft LinkedIn Group rules
LinkedIn allows Group owners to draft a policy that contains the rules that they want the Group to follow. It is important to create Group rules that are firm and clear, so as to keep an air of professionalism and make the Group as good as it can be. Reiterate the rules to anyone who violates them and hint at them in your welcome email.

Bonus Tip: Use your welcome email to push information about your websites, blog, other social media profiles, etc.

Pre-approve LinkedIn Group members
LinkedIn allows Group owners to pre-approve every member who attempts to join your Group. While it does take extra time and effort, it is a great way to ensure the ongoing quality of your Group community. If you require certain criteria for members, make this clear in your welcome email.

Use LinkedIn Group announcements
LinkedIn Group Announcements is a feature that allows you to send one announcement per week directly to the email inboxes of all your members. This is the perfect opportunity to share new content, encourage people to visit your website and blog, invite them to an event or webinar, or anything else you think will benefit them and foster more brand loyalty.

Do remember to craft a compelling subject line, to make sure your email is opened amongst all of the other LinkedIn notifications and other emails people receive every day.

Be active in leading the LinkedIn Group
As the owner of a LinkedIn Group, it is important that you maintain an active role in discussions and position yourself as its thought leader. Do not expect the Group to lead itself. Tips for keeping things ticking over nicely include posting a weekly discussion or question (with a LinkedIn Poll, perhaps), commenting on existing discussions, and encouraging engagement through questions and feedback requests.

Direct your Group members to reputable sources of information that are relevant to them and to specific discussions in order to build relationships and credibility. Don't ever use LinkedIn Groups to blatantly pitch for sales, as you run the risk of turning away potential prospects. LinkedIn, like other social networks, doesn't fit well with direct, hard selling.

Company and Showcase Pages: monitor and tweak performance with Content Marketing Score and Trending Content

In order to gain a clear insight into the performance of your paid and organic content on LinkedIn, keep an eye on your Content Marketing Score, a feature first introduced in April 2014. It measures reach and engagement with your Company Pages, LinkedIn Groups, employee updates, Sponsored updates, and more. It then gives you a single score, ranked against your competition, and provides recommendations about how to improve your score. To drill down the information for more detailed insights, you can filter your Content Marketing Score by location, company size, industry, and more. If you want to get the best idea of how your LinkedIn marketing is helping you reach your social media goals, use your Content Marketing Score in conjunction with the rest of the site's analytics tools.

Meanwhile, Trending Content is a tool that ranks all of the issues that resonate most with specific audiences on LinkedIn by their levels of sharing and engagement. Use Trending Content as a way to help tailor the content you post to be as effective and relevant as possible.

Company and Showcase Pages: LinkedIn paid advertising basics

To boost the visibility and reach of your best posts from your Company and Showcase page updates on LinkedIn, you might want to experiment with paid advertising. One of the options that makes most sense for brands is Sponsored Updates, which you can use to target content towards specific audiences based on location, job title and category, company name and category, and more. In order to make your ad spend as valuable as possible, spend a little time to anchor your Sponsored Updates with an eye-grabbing headline and a click-worthy link. Alternatively, Recommendation Ads allow you to promote your products and services to your own target market. These ad campaigns can help you increase engagement with your Company Page by bringing in more traffic and product recommendations. Each time someone recommends your product, it is automatically shared with that person's followers - which can help to keep the cycle of engagement and recommendations ticking over organically.

Once a promotion is live, visit your Company and Showcase page's analytics to see how it performs. And, as always, start with a small budget and use these insights to experiment with different styles and combinations of posts to figure out which gets you the most engagement, clicks, followers, etc., optimizing your strategy as you move forward.

YouTube Tips:
Video Made the Marketing Star

YouTube is the world's most popular online destination for video creation and sharing, and it is absolutely fantastic as a marketing tool. Faster internet speeds - and faster lives in general - mean that video is one of the dominant ways in which people want to digest information , whether that be on a desktop, tablet, or mobile device. Using the power of video in conjunction with other social media outlets to show your business off to the world has countless benefits, and this chapter will show you how to reap the rewards with YouTube.

Choose an optimum YouTube URL, link your account to Google+

Choose a YouTube username that reflects your brand for your channel URL - preferably not too long or complicated, and one that represents the name of your company or product. You will then be able to send people to this memorable address, e.g. "http://www.youtube.com/user/yourcompanyname."

Your username will default as your channel title, but you may want to change this for SEO purposes, or - as YouTube will ask for all new accounts - reflect the name associated with a Google+ profile or business page. Having a public identity that is consistent across Google will allow you to optimize your sharing, content distribution, content discovery, channel management, and more. This public identity is managed through Google+.

Note: If you have an existing YouTube channel that you want to link to Google+, go to your account settings on YouTube and click "Link channel with Google+" below your email address.

Create an engaging YouTube profile and description

Don't ignore your YouTube account's "About" section. Use it to sell your channel and its benefits to potential subscribers, and include all relevant social media and web links. Fill out a keyword-rich description that will tell people all about your channel, what they will gain from it, why they should subscribe, what your upload schedule is, etc. This text will be picked up by search engines and help your channel to rank higher in search results. The first 45 or so characters of your description will be visible when your YouTube channel appears in the "Channels" sub-section of the site's search results, so pack it with keyword-rich information.

Fill out your Channel Keywords

When people search YouTube, the site does not just return individual videos for people to watch, it also suggests whole channels that a viewer might be interested in. So, in the Advanced section of your account's Channel Settings, be sure to fill in the Channel Keywords section with keywords relevant to your channel. Think about the types of search terms that your viewers will be using and be sure to throw them in.

Associate your website with your YouTube channel

Visit your Channel Settings' "Advanced" menu again and you'll see an option to associate your channel with a website. Doing so will help YouTube to improve the quality of its search results and verify your channel as the official representation of your brand on the site. Enter your website URL and verify that you own it via the options listed, including an HTML tag or through Google Analytics.

Brand your YouTube channel background and add a high-res avatar image

Upload a square, high-resolution (1600 × 1600 pixel) profile photo that is recognizable at smaller resolutions. This avatar will be your channel's billboard all over YouTube, including in search results and comments. If you have chosen to link your Google+ account and YouTube channel, your Google+ profile or company page profile photo will have automatically become your YouTube avatar. If you want to change your profile image on YouTube, you will need to edit it via Google+, but be patient as the update might take a while to appear.

Optimize your YouTube banner art for all devices

In June 2013, YouTube rolled out a new channel layout called the One Channel design. This new look enables consistent branding across all devices (desktops, mobiles, televisions, etc.), allows you to reach out to non-subscribed viewers via a channel 'trailer' and shows off more of your content to existing subscribers to keep them watching for longer.

The One Channel layout's main branding opportunity consists of just one main banner that features your channel's profile photo to the left, and links to the channel's website and social media profiles on the right. YouTube recommends uploading an image that is 2560×1140 pixels in size. Inside this massive space are sections that cater to different screen sizes. For instance, the whole image will be seen on large televisions, while a central section of 1546×425 pixels is the 'safe' area where your logo will be visible on all devices. Whatever your design, do your best to feature your brand's personality in the channel art. Make the audience feel like they are connecting with a person or character when they arrive at your channel; this is a tactic that will encourage them to stick around.

Free YouTube One Channel banner template

To make creating your desired YouTube banner photo as easy as possible, I have built a free template for use with Adobe Photoshop or GIMP. Once you have downloaded the template, follow the instructions within it to insert your design, then save the file as a .png ready for upload to YouTube. Grab your free template via the link in the *Free Social Media Templates* chapter of this book.

Create a trailer for your YouTube channel

On the YouTube One Channel layout, you can show a trailer that will only appear (and autoplay!) to people who are not already subscribed to your channel. This is the perfect chance for you to let viewers know what your channel is all about and tell them why they should subscribe. Keep it short and to the point, eye-catching - and include a clear call to action, inviting your audience to subscribe. My trailer is about 30 seconds long, and I used the simple tools at Animoto.com to create a snazzy video that far outperforms anything I could have created alone with my limited video editing skills. If you're like me, I'd certainly recommend giving the site a look.

One other thing I love about channel trailers is that a good portion of the video's description is displayed adjacent to them. Use this space to describe what you and your channel have to offer, and don't forget to include relevant hyperlinks (shortened using tools such as bit.ly so that they are not cut off, as they will be if they are too long) and a call to action too.

To add a channel trailer, you must enable the Browse tab on your One Channel layout. The Browse tab lets you customize the display of your content. If enabled, this will be your default tab for all visitors. To enable the Browse tab:

1. Hover your cursor over the menu bar that contains the 'Video', 'About', and 'Discussion' tabs on your Channel Page.
2. Click on the pencil icon that appears and select 'Edit navigation'.

3. From here, click the button to enable the Browse feed, and then click Save.

When you re-visit your channel page, you will see a channel trailer placeholder and a '+ Channel trailer' button. Select this to choose to embed your channel trailer (which you must have already have uploaded). If you do not want a channel trailer or are in the process of making one, you can choose any existing video to sit in its place.

Set up a Fan Finder video ad for free exposure
Fan Finder is a YouTube service that promises to find and connect your channel to new viewers at no cost to you. When Fan Finder spots a potential fan, it shows an ad promoting your channel before another video plays in the hopes of encouraging them to click over and become a new, loyal viewer. Fan Finder videos must be 2 minutes or less in length. Best practices include quickly introducing your channel and hooking people in (don't assume people will have heard of your channel before and remember that they can skip the ad after the first 5 seconds has played). Entertain the viewer with teasers relevant to your content, include a strong call to action to explain why they should subscribe, and make sure your branding is clear and repeated throughout. This way, even if the viewer does not click through, it gives the best chance possible that they will remember your channel and visit on their own accord in future.

To set up a Fan Finder video, visit https://www.youtube.com/fan_finder. You can choose any of your uploaded videos to be your Fan Finder video as long as it is two minutes or less in length. My advice is to create a custom advert or - if you're a bit pressed for time - simply use your channel trailer as an easy and effective substitute.

Create playlists and sections to group and feature your content

Build playlists and feature your best content in them, to encourage multiple video views in one session, and to organize your content for viewers. Consider creating a playlist of your most popular videos too.

Create a playlist in the One Channel YouTube layout

The One Channel YouTube layout allows you to take greater control over how you present your videos and playlists on your channel. You can organize content into highly visible sections for your fans to discover what to watch. With multiple layouts for videos and playlists, you can arrange your channel to best highlight your content. To add sections to your channel, click the 'Add section' button below your channel's trailer. From here, use the drop-down menus to choose the content you want to display (Recent Uploads, Likes, Popular Content, etc.) and how you want it laid out - either in a horizontal row or as a vertical list. To edit or remove an existing section, hover your mouse over the videos within it and click the pencil icon that appears. From here, make any changes - or click the garbage can icon to delete the section completely.

Tips for YouTube video making and optimization

Find your company's cheerleader and use screen capturing

Who is the cheeriest person in your office? Consider them to front your YouTube videos, as they'll appeal to your audience. Everyone shy about being on camera? If you don't have anyone who wants to be the face of your business, consider something like Google Search Stories (http://www.youtube.com/user/SearchStories) to show off your best online properties or if, like me, you do a lot of web demonstrations, use screen capturing software such as Camtasia (expensive but great quality and editing options) or

Screenr (completely free, but without editing features). *Ideally*, you want to have a person in front of camera, or a mix of screen capture and someone onscreen, as this approach will resonate with your audience best.

Find the correct tone of voice

Your tone of voice in a video is very important. Remember, it's a conversation you're having, so avoid the cheesy radio announcer voice and speak naturally. When expressing yourself on video, be real. Robotic speech or blatantly reading from a script will not appeal to viewers. Talk directly to your fans as if you're in a room with them; it couldn't get much more personal than that.

Hook viewers with a teaser or intrigue

With low viewer attention spans and YouTube making it so easy for them to click away to someone else's content, it is crucial to use the opening seconds of your video to hook viewers in and keep them watching *your* recordings until the end. This portion of your video only needs to be a few seconds long, but its effectiveness can pay dividends towards watch time and viewer engagement. Examples include:

- Showing off the finished result in a "how to" video and telling your audience that this is what they'll have learned to create by the end of your clip.
- Offering a mysterious line or quip like, *"What is the link between a potato and unbelievable sales conversion? Keep watching to find out..."*

Keep video length short and content relevant

YouTube viewers are not going to sit and watch an infomercial for 20 minutes. If you saw two videos offering exactly the same information - one 3 minutes long and the other 20 minutes long, which would you click on? Aim for 1-2 minutes ideally and 3-5 minutes max. Similarly, keep your content relevant, especially in relation to your video's title and custom thumbnail (more on both of these coming up). Know what message you want to communicate in your video and stick to it; too much waffling and you'll lose your audience in a second.

Keep video intro titles short (or get rid of them altogether)
How many videos do you stop watching because of long and boring introductions featuring pointless graphics and awful music? Jump straight into the action to keep viewers hooked or, if necessary, at least keep your intro graphics short and snappy, explaining who you are and what the video is all about.

Plan your greeting and sign off
Start every video with a greeting, your name, and business name. Finish with your business name and tag line. I do this for all my videos as they act as two little plugs for this book, and also encourage users to 'Click the subscribe button' to tempt more subscribers and guarantee future views. My YouTube intro and sign-offs are as follows:

Intro: *Hello everybody, it's Andrew here again, author of 500 Social Media Marketing Tips; check out the link in the description to grab your copy today. In this video, I'm going to show you...*

Sign Off: *That's all for this time, I hope it helped. Don't forget to click 'subscribe' for lots more social media marketing tips like this one, to give me a like if you enjoyed this video - and to check out the link to my book in the description below. Thanks very much for watching, and good bye!*

Feature call to actions within your videos
Depending on where during the video would be most effective, include calls to action (CTAs) to direct your viewers - do you want them to visit your website, call you for a quote, watch another video, reply to a question in the comments, subscribe for more

great content, click an annotation or the link in the description? Tell them! CTAs can be implemented in several ways, including direct from the video host, as clickable annotations or in on-screen graphics. For example, at the end of each of my videos, I have an end card that features a teaser of my previous video (clickable via a spotlight annotation), and calls to action that encourage viewers to "like" the video they have just watched, and encouraging them to subscribe to my channel.

Use annotations to drive interactivity, revitalize old content, and drive web traffic

Where relevant, feature annotations in your YouTube videos that add value, a bit like the way stats and information is displayed onscreen during a sports game on television. Access the Annotations tool on your Video Manager page. Click Edit underneath the video you want to add an annotation to, then choose Annotations from the drop-down menu. Here are a few ways annotations can be used well:

Highlight nuances of details forgotten in the edit
Sometimes you'll create and publish a video, only to realize you forgot to mention one important detail that is essential to the video as a whole - d'oh! Shooting the whole thing again might be either impossible or too time-consuming, but an annotation can be used to inform viewers of the key, supplementary, info while they watch.

Revitalize old content
Using the YouTube Annotations tool is also helpful if you have created a video which, as time passes, features out-of-date info. Rather than deleting the video, create a fresh video with the updated information, then go back to the original video and embed an annotation with a call to action that takes people to the updated video page when clicked.

145

Ask for likes, comments, and subscriptions

One of the most popular uses for annotations is to ask for video likes, comments, or subscriptions. It can be an effective tactic and it's one I employ myself - but I would recommend leaving these types of annotations until the end of your videos. Bombarding viewers at the start or throughout your videos with these types of messages is, at best, distracting - and at worse can be enough to put people off you and your channel completely.

Create Associated website annotations

Associated website annotations enable you to add a clickable link to a non-YouTube URL within the video player itself. They work great for branding purposes, and as an easy way to direct people either audibly or visually to click through to your website. Here's how to set one up:

1. Verify ownership of your YouTube account by telephone at http://www.youtube.com/verify
2. Add your website as an associated website and verify ownership of it via Google Webmaster Tools - visit https://www.google.com/webmasters/tools to do this. You'll need backend access to your site to add some code, so contact your web developer if you need help here.
3. Back on your YouTube Video Manager page, visit the "Advanced" section of the Channel Settings menu. Here, add your website URL to the box next to "Associated website." When confirmed, a green "Success" circle will appear.
4. You're done! When adding an annotation to your videos, choose the Associated Website type from the drop-down menu, and add your full website URL into the box provided.

Annotation duration, size, color, placement, number, & text
Duration

146

Although annotations can be closed manually by a viewer (by hovering over them and clicking the X), remove any potential hindrance by only displaying your annotations for as long as it takes to read them. Adjust the length of time an annotation displays, using the slidebar in the Annotations tool. YouTube recommends that, in most cases, 5-7 seconds is sufficient enough time for most annotations to be read and understood or clicked.

Size

Just because your annotations can take up the whole of the video player doesn't mean that they should! Try to make them as small as possible so that they are as subtle as they need to be and block as little of your video content as has to be covered. Also, as with almost every area of the Internet, WRITING YOUR ANNOTATIONS IN CAPS may be considered shouting or rude, so it is best avoided.

Color

If your annotation is critical to the theme or message of your video, then filling them in bright and eye-catching colors such as yellow, blue, orange, red or pink could be the way forward. Otherwise, however, annotations need not be the center of attention, and more muted colors such as grey, white, black - or even the transparent option - work best. Whichever background fill color you use, make sure that the text color contrasts with it so that your annotation is easily read.

Placement

Avoid placing annotations in the lower third of your videos. The advertisement overlay can obscure annotations placed there, and an embedded YouTube video can also obstruct annotations along the very top of the frame. Try to position them away from the very center of the video, where they can be distracting. The left and right sidebars are a good option.

Number

YouTube recommends using the fewest number of annotations necessary in any given video. They also suggest that you avoid displaying two annotations at the same time, as this can be distracting for viewers. However, in instances at the end of a video where, for example, you are asking viewers to click an annotation to subscribe to your channel, hit 'like' or view another video, I think this advice can be somewhat overlooked.

Type

Choose the most appropriate type of annotation to use in your video. Title annotations, because of their size, are useful for adding headings at the beginning of your video. Notes and Labels are good for briefly highlighting important points or adding a quick call to action, Then there's Speech Bubbles: many people use these as a way to 'point' to buttons that exist around the video on the YouTube website (Like, subscribe, comment, etc.). However, these annotations will make no sense to anyone watching if the video is embedded on a website or in full-screen. The best use for Speech Bubbles is as a whimsical way to add thoughts or speech to characters in your video.

Watermark your YouTube videos

Add a company watermark and/or URL to your videos for authenticity, and to show off your brand name if the video is embedded elsewhere. You can either do this in your video editor before you upload your completed recording, or consider adding a clickable annotation to your YouTube videos - as in the InVideo Programming feature detailed in the next tip - which serves a similar purpose and can also encourage views and subscribers.

Add InVideo Programming for branding

YouTube introduced a great little tool for marketers in October

2012 called InVideo Programming. It allows you to add a Featured Video or Featured Channel clickable image annotation (or both) to all of your videos at once - a great strategy for reinforcing branding and driving up views. To access and set it up, click on Channel Settings within Video Manager and choose the InVideo Programming option. An effective strategy I have employed is to create an InVideo Programming watermark that is a call to action. Mine is an image that reads 'FREE Social Media Tutorials' and sits in the corner of all my videos. When clicked, it takes people to my Channel page and acts as a way to encourage them to view more content and to subscribe. Another smart idea is to set your InVideo Programming featured video annotation to appear around the time in your videos where (using your YouTube analytics for reference) you notice that a lot of your audience disengages with your content and moves on. The goal is to keep them watching your stuff, even if it's a different video entirely!

Post videos regularly and consistently
Once you launch a YouTube account and publish your first video, don't just abandon your account. Try staying regular by making at least one or two videos per week, to build traction with your audience and have them look forward to your new content. If you can't be around to post a video manually, use the feature to schedule your upload for posting ahead of time - this option is available from the drop-down menu on the video upload page.

YouTube video title SEO
When coming up with a title for your videos, think about what your audience is likely to search for and reflect that in the words that you use. Your video title should be keyword rich and *match* the content that your content contains. Only the first ~45 characters of your video title are displayed in the YouTube search results on mobile devices, so make sure you front-end load the title with your

149

primary keyword phrase(s). Here are some quick pointers to help get even more from your video headings:

- Use deliberate capitalization of words to highlight your content, e.g. 'The Top 10 Reasons Facebook Marketing Works' instead of 'The top 10 reason Facebook marketing works'.
- Add colon after your initial keywords and rephrase your title. For example, your video on saving money "How to Save Money: The Saving Money Plan." This will help capture those people who are searching for videos by using two similar (but different) phrases.
- Make your title's catchy in a way that will encourage users to click. For example, in a video that teaches people how to tie a bow tie - and do it in 30 seconds or less - which of the following would be more appealing: "How to Tie A Bow Tie" or "How to Tie A Bow Tie in 30 Seconds or Less."

Write effective video descriptions
Write a tempting and teasing description that makes the potential viewer want to hit the play button when they see it in search results - such as adding a five-to-six word call to action, e.g. "*Lose 4lb this week easily!*" Or start your description with a full URL to your company's website. Don't be stingy with the rest of the space you have either. Be as descriptive and keyword-rich as possible to help your search ranking - but don't be spammy or repeat keywords unnecessarily.

Keep the most important keyword phrases near the beginning of your description because the text that is visible on your video's page (above the "Show More" button) has more value to search engines than text hidden below it. This initial snippet of description text is also what will appear in search results.

Note: When adding links in your video description, type out the entire URL to your website, including the "http://" prefix, so that

YouTube will automatically hyperlink it. Otherwise, people won't be able to click through to your site.

Select the right video category

Make sure that you submit your YouTube video to the right category - choose the one that your viewers are most likely to look under to find your content. If there is no exact match (and there often isn't), choose the category that most closely fits your upload. Videos submitted in irrelevant categories may not get relevant traffic, so this step is important. If your video could fit into two categories, select the one where you think it might have least competition to increase the chances of it being found or even featured.

Tag your video effectively

Include keyword tags for each video that are relevant to the video and your business, to make sure it can be found in a YouTube search as easily as possible. The more relevant your tags, the more discoverable your video will be. Use as many different tags as necessary. To help you come up with tags, think about the different keywords that viewers will search find your video; if your video was split into sections or themes, how would you describe them in a single word or phrase? Always keep them on topic and always provide enough tags to thoroughly and accurately describe the video content. There is no perfect number of tags, but they should always be topically accurate and concise. To boost your video's search ranking, use quotation marks to isolate important keyword phrases with multiple words, e.g. "how to make a paper airplane", as well as typing the phrase without the punctuation.

Create a custom video thumbnail (or choose the best default option)

Thumbnails act as mini marketing posters for your content and are important in attracting viewers to your videos wherever they are seen - either on YouTube, in Google search results or embedded on websites. Assuming your account is in good standing, you may have the option to upload a thumbnail once your video has uploaded. If the feature isn't enabled (mine took a good few months to appear) be patient as you can always go back and add them in later. In the meantime, you can choose the best option from a default selection of three thumbnail images that YouTube offers you after your content is uploaded.

If you are able to create your own, one tactic I often employ is to use the thumbnail to double-up on the impact of a great video title. For example, if I had a video entitled *"How to Write A Great YouTube Title"*, I would create a thumbnail image with the same phrase written on it in a big, bold font and a contrasting background so that it stands out from all competing videos in YouTube's search results. The ideal size to create a YouTube thumbnail in a photo editor is 1280 × 720 pixels, so that it appears crisp and clear across the site, whichever device it is viewed on.

The general guidelines YouTube recommends for thumbnails are:

- Clear, in-focus, hi-resolution (640 × 360 pixels min, 16:9 aspect ratio)
- Bright, high-contrast
- Close-ups of faces
- Visually compelling imagery
- Well-framed, good composition
- Foreground stands out from background
- Looks great at both small and large sizes.
- Accurately represents the content.

Save time with video info defaults
If you find yourself uploading much the same video info (tags, description, title, etc.) each time, set video info defaults for these to

automatically appear in Channel Settings > Defaults to save yourself some time. Create a set of 'standard tags' for your channel that can be applied to any video you publish on YouTube, e.g. filmmaking, animation, comedy, "Funny Videos", "Pet Videos", etc. Actively update and optimize archived videos with relevant tags when new search trends emerge.

YouTube video ideas for Business

Interview experts at trade shows

To spread your reputation as an industry expert, interview your peers at trade events that you attend and film these interactions to create a YouTube video afterwards (make sure to get permission from the subject and event organizer first, though). It's a great form of marketing, particularly if the interviewee is popular and well respected, and links to your video after you've posted it online. You could even get someone to interview you - you're an expert in your field, right? Easy, powerful video content for you right there!

Create a video series

One-off videos are all well and good, but a planned series of videos will keep viewers engaged over a number of days or weeks. Make sure to tell them that your video is part of a series (visually, in the title (e.g. *How to Knit A Winter Scarf: Part 1*) and audibly (e.g. *"This is part one of your guide to knitting a warm scarf for winter"*) and encourage them to subscribe to come back for more. A series is also useful for chopping what might be one long video into separate, shorter, more viewable chunks.

Be funny, weird, and useful

The most popular videos on YouTube are ones that make people laugh, so give it a go. People are more likely to share something funny too.

Create content that addresses your audience's needs. 'How to' videos are a great way to do this - use your expertise! Think about the how-to ideas your customers are looking for and create videos to help. Funny and useful are two of the most popular shareable video types, and weird content is the third most shareable. If it works for your brand, look into producing something off-the-wall that will resonate with your audience.

Record product demos and reviews

Rather than *telling* people what your product or service can do, why not *show* them instead? Product demo videos are a great way to demonstrate your wares to customers. Alternatively, record videos of product reviews - not necessarily of your own products, but those your customers will be interested in. For popular examples as proof of how this strategy works, search YouTube for stuff like reviews of iPads, vacuum cleaners, gym equipment or any type of consumer goods.

Show viewers around, upload presentations and talks

Take your audience on a tour of your offices and city to help them feel connected with you and your brand; give them a sneak peek behind the scenes. Upload recordings of presentations you've given, to demonstrate your authority within your business niche, and to show off your public speaking skills.

Ask your audience to review and promote your products

Ask your audience to use your product in their videos (like product placement in movies), or to provide reviews, and cross-promote each other. You can then feature these customer-created videos on other social networking sites to increase your exposure, and play to the vanity of your customers, who will love to see themselves featured on your pages.

Ask and answer questions for your audience

One of the best ways to get and keep your audience engaged on YouTube is to ask questions for them to answer or ask them to submit questions for you to reply to. For the former, ask viewers to submit a comment or record and link to a video response. For the latter ask fans to leave a comment featuring a question for a chance to see it answered in your next video or, even better, to video record themselves asking the question which they then email to you so that you can feature it in your next upload. Imagine how surprised and delighted a customer will feel if you show off their feedback in a video, rather than just respond to it via a reply in the comments.

Announcements and community service

Do you have key dates or occasions in your business' life? Mark them with a video and thank your customers for their support, e.g. your 1000th customer or 100th video.

Highlight the causes your organization cares about and the philanthropy you carry out in the local community - make videos that show you care.

News and views - be timely and topical

Are you in a dynamically moving industry? Show your expertise by making videos to announce and discuss breaking news and information. React to trending topics in your niche with relevant content when it makes sense for your audience. Being part of what's going viral, rising search trends or breaking news can be critical for certain content. News and politics, sports, commentary, and opinion content can thrive on topicality.

Collaborate, study the competition

- Look into collaborating with other YouTube channel owners in order to share audiences, introducing each other to subscribers and sharing complementary content. As well as appearing in each other's videos, you can feature any playlist from another channel as a section on your own channel by selecting the "Enter a playlist URL" option when setting one up.

- One of the best ways to see what will work for your business on YouTube is to study other popular videos of the type that you want to create, and use them as inspiration.

Convert podcasts into YouTube videos

Does your company have a podcast? Turn them into videos and upload them to YouTube to expand your reach. You can also use the script for your videos to create a podcast feed and submit it to iTunes, which has an audience of hundreds of millions of people. To get the very best exposure on iTunes, create an eye-catching graphic and a keyword-rich description for your content.

Increasing views on your YouTube videos

Ask for likes and comments

YouTube videos that get plenty of views, 'likes' and comments rank higher in its searches, so ask users to click that thumbs-up button, either audibly or through annotations.

Extending video impact strategy

Here's a quick tip to compound the impact of a new video: 'Like' and 'favorite' the video on your channel after a timely increment (for example, 24 hours later) to make it reappear in your subscribers' "All Activity" home page feed, and give them another chance to see it if they missed it first time around.

Use the feed to engage viewers

The feed broadcasts your YouTube channel activities to your current subscribers. By default the feed includes uploads, liked videos, videos added to playlists, bulletins, comments you make, channels to which you subscribe, and 'favorited' videos. Adjust your sharing settings to set the appropriate feed strategy for your channel and subscriber interests. If you do not upload regularly, the feed allows an easy way to appear active by broadcasting your other activities on the site. Space out your interactions on YouTube. Multiple actions get aggregated into a single post for your subscribers, so maximize their impact as individual posts, by leaving time in between.

Post a bulletin to your subscribers

A bulletin is a text update you send from your Channel page to all of your subscribers. You can tell your subscribers about a video you're working on, remind them of an awesome video you posted recently or include a link to a video you recommend, with a comment about it. When you post a bulletin, it will appear on your subscribers' recent activity feed (on their homepages) and on your Channel page in your recent activity feed. Here's how to post a bulletin:

1. Sign into your YouTube account
2. Go to your Channel page
3. When viewing your Feed underneath the 'Browse videos' tab you will see a 'Create a new post' text field box. Enter your bulletin's text, add a video or playlist link to share (optional) and click 'Post'
4. Your bulletin will then be sent out to your subscribers.

Blog about your videos

Every time you post a new video, compose a blog post based around it, and share it with your fans and followers and social media. Conversely, if you write a blog post that is particularly visual and would work well as a video, then why not screen grab it while you talk through it and turn the blog post into content for your YouTube channel? I often use this strategy for step-by-step guides, and as a bonus the blog text sitting right in front of me is a helpful reminder of what I want to say!

Embed a YouTube Subscribe widget on your blog or website
A YouTube Subscribe widget is a little box that you can embed in the sidebar of your website to encourage people to subscribe to your channel, or click through to check it out. It displays your YouTube channel icon, subscriber count, the number of videos you have published and, of course, an all-important Subscribe button. What I like about it most is that it acts as a permanent advertisement for your video content. I combine my widget with an embedded playlist that displays my most recently-published video to compound its effectiveness.

For a look at a YouTube Subscribe widget, further instructions, and the code needed to embed one on your own website, visit the following link: http://bit.ly/youtubesubscribewidget

Leverage other social media to increase reach
- Post your video to Facebook, (making sure to choose the best thumbnail).
- Tweet about it on Twitter with a couple of relevant hashtags (also include the prefix "Video:" before the video title, as although a shortened YouTube URL will show, it may not always be immediately obvious to your followers that you're sharing visual content - something they are more likely to engage with.
- Pin your video to Pinterest and make sure that the video's title and a short description is posted along with it, as well as a couple of relevant hashtags. All of these details will improve the chances of your content being found by others in Pinterest search.
- Consider submitting your video to other major video sharing sites such as Dailymotion and Vimeo. These sites might not have the massive popularity of YouTube, but it could be that your most lucrative customers only ever browse those video websites. Also submit your video to StumbleUpon. This social bookmarking site has always been a powerful referrer.

Comment on other videos

Whenever you leave a comment on another video, your username and avatar will be visible to everybody on that page, driving more traffic to your videos. Always comment in a way that will reflect well on your brand. Be helpful, insightful or funny and aim to become a well 'thumbed-up' comment that appears for a significant amount of time in the 'Top Comments' section.

Manage comments effectively

Be sure to keep a tab on the comments being left on your video via the Community option, found in the Video Manager portion of your account. Let commenters on your videos know that you appreciate what they have to say, and respond as often as you can. They'll appreciate the time you give to do so. Don't go deleting any negative ones without reply, but do see that your brand isn't being unduly damaged. If you expect a great number of comments, at least try to be around for the first hour or two after publishing so that you can respond to immediate feedback.

YouTube began a roll out of a much-improved commenting system in late 2013. Here is a summary of the major changes; I'm sure you can pick out the benefits:

Comments ranked by importance: Posts from the video's creator (you!), popular personalities, engaged discussions about the video, and people in your Google+ Circles rise to the top of the comment list underneath the video.

Private or public conversations: Choose to start a conversation so that it is seen by everyone on YouTube and Google+, only people in your Circles or just one person. Replies are threaded so you can easily follow conversations.

Improved moderating tools: Review comments before they're posted, block certain words or auto-approve comments from certain fans to save time and allow more opportunities to share videos and connect with your fans.

Subtitle all your videos
It might take a little longer, but adding transcripts for your videos to make them accessible to the hearing impaired shows that you really care about your customers; crucially, the text is picked up by Google and helps greatly in the ranking of your video in its web search. You can edit YouTube's automatically-generated captions from any video page.

Edit your videos nicely, grab FREE YouTube Music
If you're serious about videos as a social media tool, consider investing in some decent video editing software and learn to perfect your craft. Otherwise, Windows Movie Maker for PC and iMovie for Mac are adequate enough for most needs. If you have a decent HD camera, be sure that its audio is just as good - stand close to the camera if you don't have a dedicated microphone. People don't often expect YouTube content to have Hollywood production values, so although you should aim for the best output as possible, prepare to accept a little less than perfect.

In September 2013, the YouTube Audio Library was launched. It is a brilliant tool for those of you who want to use the power of music to add emotion and depth to the video content you create, or just a simple backing track - and it won't cost you a penny. The library features hundreds of royalty-free instrumental tracks (arranged by mood, genre, instrument and duration) that you can use for free, forever, for any creative purpose (not just in your YouTube videos). Access it via a link on your Video Manager page.

Experiment with YouTube ads

You can bid on keywords for pennies on YouTube ads, cheap as chips compared to what you pay for a Google text ad, or even a Facebook ad. Visit the following link to get started: http://www.youtube.com/yt/advertise/index.html

Review YouTube Analytics often

You can gather so much useful information on an individual video or on all the videos you've uploaded in YouTube Analytics. See what is working best and adjust your strategy accordingly - e.g. do some types of videos get more views and better engagement than others? Are your videos being found via YouTube or other sites? Which is your most liked video, etc.? To access your YouTube Analytics, click the 'Analytics' button at the top of your Channel page when you are signed in.

Instagram Tips:
Snap-happy Marketing Strategy

Instagram, the fun and quirky image app, has taken the world by storm since launching in October 2010. Hundreds of millions of people use Instagram as a way to transform everyday photos and videos with filters and frames, into memory-laden content, which can then be shared with the world. Chances are that snaps and recordings of your brand are already on Instagram, and all of this content acts as authentic peer-to-peer endorsements of you - essentially free advertising. With a sound strategy of your own, you can only help to compound this effect, increasing brand loyalty and driving sales as a result. Some have even dubbed Instagram "The World's Most Powerful Selling Tool," such is the level of passion and engagement that its users show. This chapter is split into five sections to help you get the most from the app:

- Using Instagram for Business
- Gaining Followers on Instagram
- Taking Great Instagram Photos
- How to Record Video With Instagram
- How to Use Instagram Direct for Business

Note: While this chapter references Instagram throughout, many of the tips can apply to *any* method of photo-sharing on social media (e.g. uploading images to Facebook and Twitter), as well as micro-video apps such as Vine and Snapchat, which are discussed in other chapters of this book.

Using Instagram for Business

Understand the "culture of Instragram"

The top-performing brands on Instagram all have one thing in common: they understand what makes the app unique compared to other social networks, and use this knowledge to their advantage. While the definition of "Instagram culture" will inevitably change over time, at its core are users who are *proud* of the content they post - you won't see hundreds of impulsive selfies and blurry night club photos from the most popular "artists", for instance. As such, there is a definite lean towards quality over quantity, which sees creators taking their time to carefully compose and construct photos and videos, cropping and editing until they are just right so that when an item does eventually get posted to their Instagram feed, it is poured over by impressed followers, complimented with lots of likes and comments, and attracts new fans (*"Wow, these guys post great stuff and get a lot of love; I'm sticking around for more!"*) in the process. One of Instagram's central mantras is to encourage people to "find beauty everywhere." For businesses, this means showing how your company sees the world, sharing imagery that pushes people's ideas of you deeper than the common perception, and offering a view into the lifestyle that your product or service makes possible both through your own eyes and those of customers who use them.

In short, whereas visual imagery for sites like Facebook and Twitter might sometimes be more ad-hoc in nature or Pinterest more simple and mood board-y or salesy, your preference on Instagram should be more creative, arty, and *special*, with even more of an emphasis on visual storytelling. Immerse yourself in the culture of Instagram by reflecting this more imaginative style of photos or videos in your own feed (clearly expressing a defined personality and voice and mirroring the attitude and preferences of app's majority audience), and you'll be in a significantly powerful position from the get go.

Promote new products and offers

As with all social networks, Instagram offers you a way of promoting new products, services and offers through images and a photo caption featuring a description of the product, a call to action, and a customized, short URL that can be used to access it. URLs written within Instagram descriptions cannot be clicked on, so making links here short and memorable is essential. Keep in mind that users do not follow brands on Instagram to be given a hard sell every day, so balance such photos with other types of posts, as described below.

To make the most of the relatively small real estate of mobile devices, make a habit of focusing in on particular details of products or service in order to draw customers in. For example, a clothing store might highlight the quality dye and material in a garment, while a decorating service could go a bit more abstract and use the close-up shot of a pot of paint and a brush to represent a job well done.

Feature customers using your products, and "piggyback"
There is no better promotion for your business to new customers than to show photos of existing customers enjoying what you offer, so take advantage of this using Instagram. Take snaps from inside your store, restaurant or business; re-purpose images submitted to you by happy customers. For example, pen manufacturer Sharpie regularly features sketches drawn by its customers, and Starbucks "piggybacks" on the popularity of Instagram users with large follow bases, reposting images (with permission, of course) that feature their products.

Show behind the scenes
To increase intimacy with your brand and make customers feel that they are getting a special sneak peek at the inner workings of your brand, use Instagram to snap photos of behind-the-scenes goings-on at your company. For example, Tiffany & Co once snapped a

photo of an artist they had employed, right in the middle of him painting a new backdrop for its new Fifth Avenue store.

Highlight your charitable side

To help enhance your brand image, use Instagram images to highlight your charitable side. Levis regularly promotes the good its company does, such as posting a photo of a t-shirt printed for the free day it gives all employees so that they can help projects in their local communities.

Ask questions

Like all social networks, one of the best ways to interact with fans and gather their thoughts and feedback (which you can then use to tailor future Instagram content or business offerings), is to ask questions. You can either post an image or video and ask the question underneath in its caption, overlay the question with text in the image or recording itself, or simply ask it aloud during a recording. For apps to help you do this easily, see advice later on in this chapter. Brands like Mastercard and Chevrolet have used this strategy to great effect in the past, with questions like *"Got a great photo of Miami? Tag it #LoveThisCity! We want to see your best pics!"* and *"How do you explain the rush behind the wheel of a new #Camaro?"* respectively. Both encourage their fans to react and get involved with things they are passionate about, i.e. their hometown and their car. In the case of Mastercard, it's by posting photos to their own feeds that will associate the user with the brand (which, of course, all of their own followers will see), and for Chevrolet, they get valuable feedback from genuine fans about their latest motor.

If you're simply aiming to encourage the most engagement, try "fill in the blank" (My favorite burger from Bob's Burgers is ___), yes/no (Are you a fan of Monday mornings?) or A/B (Which of these t-shirt designs do you like best? We'll print the winner starting next week!) questions as these require the least amount of effort to respond to.

Offer hints and tips

As a fun and interesting brand to follow on Instagram, offering hints and tips to your customers is a great way to be consistently valuable, increase the potential virality of your posts, and to grow brand loyalty. Two of the easiest ways to do this are to show simple step-by-step instructions, either by composing a single Instagram photo split into several frames (using apps like PicFrame or Diptic to achieve this effect), or by demonstrating the steps in a short video clip. Brands like Petsmart use single Instagram posts split into multiple images to give simple pet training advice, like teaching a dog to sit and lay. The photo instructions are complimented by further explanation in the text caption.

Hold an Instagram contest

Instagram contests are hugely popular and can provide a quick, cheap, and powerful way to encourage fans to engage with your brand, and spread the word about you across Instagram and beyond. Here are a series of simple steps to help ensure your Instagram contest is a success:

1. Choose a prize

Choose a prize that is unique to your business, e.g. a product or gift card so that you will attract entrants who are genuinely interested in your business, not just in winning an iPad or $500 cash, for example. Also, try to make the size of the prize proportionate to the effort it will take to win it, which leads us onto...

2. Decide on an entry method

Some of the simplest contest entry methods on Instagram include asking fans to like a photo, follow your account, or re-post an image (with an app like Regram or simply screen-grabbing your published photo). You can also decide to advertise a contest held elsewhere, like on your Facebook Page or your website, via your Instagram account, and drive people to those destinations via a memorable shortened URL in your image's caption or a clickable link in your Instagram bio.

Alternatively, some of the most common entry methods ask users to post a photo or a video on Instagram in order to be entered; often tied to a particular theme, e.g. food, colors, seasons, their favorite product from your range.

3. Build your contest

When you launch the contest with a post on Instagram, featuring an attention-grabbing title with a short call-to-action will help to maximize entries, e.g. *"Enter to Win a $100 Gift Card from Sean's Salon!"* A photo of the prize is a great way to entice people to enter to win it. If you're giving away a gift card, for example, include an image with the gift card value in text and a product that people can buy with it. Write the entry method and prizing info in the description - a paragraph with info about the prize, how to enter and any rules or restrictions for your contest, linked to with a short URL or a clickable link in your bio.

4. Monitor progress

To help gauge the success of your Instagram contest:

- Use hashtags to easily track how many photos are being shared on Instagram that have your contest hashtag (ask fans to use one in the caption for the photos or videos they post as a requirement for entry, but make sure beforehand that your chosen hashtag is unique and hasn't been used by someone else before).
- Set up Google Alerts to monitor mentions of your contest across the web.

- Use Wishpond or Woobox Instagram contest web apps for real-time campaign reports, which allows you to track views, entries, and conversion rates.

5. Promote your contest
In addition to organic marketing of your competition, send an email to your mailing list (these are the people most likely to enter), promote your contest on social networks, and add a banner to the home page of your website.

6. Follow-up actions
After your contest is over, follow these steps to wrap everything up neatly:
- Showcase winning photos on your Instagram account and other social channels.
- Share a video showing you choosing the winning photo to create excitement.
- Post teasers for future contests on Instagram to keep your followers hooked, keep momentum going, and prime followers for future contests on your Instagram account.
- Run regular contests on Instagram (weekly or monthly) to get fans into the habit of looking forward to them and entering.

Re-purpose Instagram content
The Instagram-style of photos is popular all over the web. To make the most of your Instagram snaps and the positive messages they relay about your brand, re-purpose the content. Share it with your Twitter, Facebook and Pinterest followers. Even if you decide not to use Instagram as part of your social media strategy, the types of photos noted above can still be used to increase the variety and quality of your social media output.

Gaining Followers on Instagram

168

Fill out your profile in full, add a profile photo that fits a circle

One of the easiest ways to connect with would-be Instagram followers is to fill out your profile in full, including a short description about who you are and what you do. And don't forget to add the URL to your website in this section too, which is clickable from your profile and could help to drive traffic.

Equally as important is to add a photo or profile yourself if you're the figurehead of your company (ideally of your smiley face) or, instead, your company logo, as this will represent you all across the service Like Google+, Instagram (on its mobile app at least) favors a circular profile photo, which suits faces better than it does company logos. If your logo is square and messily cropped when you upload it to your Instagram profile, use my free *square-logo-into-circle-fit template* as an easy fix. Grab it via the link in the Free Social Media Templates chapter of this book.

In late 2012, Instagram rolled out official web profiles for users. Login to your account; your web profile URL will be www.instagram.com/yourinstagramusername. When an Instagram image link is posted to Twitter, Facebook, Flickr, Foursquare, Tumblr and other sites, a user will be directed to your web profile when it is clicked. Web-based profiles mean that these people can comment and/or like the image direct on the web - no mobile app is required. Marketers can use this knowledge as an opportunity to promote more interaction among fans.

Only post your best photos

The best Instagram photographers are extremely picky about the images they post on their accounts - quality definitely trumps quantity where your portfolio is concerned. Take your time in creating a collection of photos that you are really proud of - your very best efforts - as it is these that will catch the eye of others.

Take several photographs before settling on your favorite, as your first effort is very rarely going to be the best.

Vary your subject matter

Taking pictures of only one type of thing - flowers, boats, clouds, etc - may be your bag, but to make your stream interesting, mix it up a little bit. Try action shots, still life, black and whites and color, faces and buildings. Check out your most recent ten photos and ask yourself, *"Do they all look the same?"*, *"Would newcomers find my portfolio interesting to view and want to follow?"*

Describe your images, ask questions

Give viewers of your photos more information about the story behind them by describing them before you post in the caption box. Tell them (or ask them to guess) where they were taken, how you produced the shots, etc. Encourage interaction!

How often should you post?

Even if you are a pro photographer, you will only annoy your followers if you post vast swathes of photos to Instagram every day, especially since they'd, in all honesty, want to see photos from their friends and family primarily. Post a few photos a day at the most to keep your followers on your side and give each of your images their own time in the spotlight. Many of the biggest brands on Instagram post just once per day, sometimes even less.

If you're really determined to build a loyal Instagram following, you must be in it for the long haul, and that means posting over an extended period of time. If you post for a few weeks and don't see the numbers racking up, don't be disheartened - slow and steady wins the race. To grow and maintain follower numbers, post regularly and don't ignore your Instagram account for weeks or months at a time.

Post at different times of the day

Even if you have selected your favorite few photos at the start of the day and are ready to share them, don't post them all at once! Instagram is a global community with people checking it out at different times throughout the day. And again, it's all about giving each photo its time to shine, by staggering your offerings over each 24-hour period.

Tag your photos, but don't be spammy

Instagram allows you to tag each photo with up to 30 hashtags, so be sure to make use of them. Tagging your photo with a hashtag will have it placed with other photos with the same tag and turned into clickable links to see said photo sets. Crucially, words in your description that are not preceded with a hashtag will *not* be taken into account when a user searches for photos, so be cautiously liberal with your efforts. An example might read *"Check out our #new selection of #gorgeous #muffins, they go great with #coffee at our #nyc branch."*

Note: If you spend even a short amount of time on Instagram, you will notice how prevalent (and perhaps over-the-top) hashtag use is. Although this helps individuals - often desperate for an audience - attract a few more views, I would not recommend so blatant a tactic for business, as it can come across as spammy, dilute your marketing message and damage your brand image. Generous use of hashtags is part of the Instagram culture - one that is even more casual that that on Facebook and Twitter - but I would still exercise caution for the reasons just listed. The competitive analysis company, Trackmaven, found that using between 4 and 5 hashtags maximized Instagram interactions, but more than 5 hashtags worsened engagement.

Make hashtags relevant and descriptive

Make it easy for other like-minded Instagrammers to find you by making sure your tags describe your photo. Using general tags like #clothes or #food might find you a few followers, but being much more specific and descriptive will provide a much better chance of being found and followed. In addition, study the most-used hashtags within your business niche and incorporate them into your own strategy.

After you've been using Instagram for a while, you're probably going to notice that you use lots of the same hashtags regularly. To make inserting them into your posts much more simple, save them in the Notes app on iPhone (or similar on Android), so that you can quickly copy and paste them into Instagram before you publish.

Geo-tag your photos on a Photo Map
Instagram allows you to geo-tag your photos with the location at which they were taken, which are then added to a Photo Map. When a photo is tagged in this way, Instagrammers who are close to your location or who visit it at a later date will be able to view your photos. The resulting affinity may lead to a follow or a visit to your store, and generally adds a greater sense of place and interest to the snap.

Note: Even if you do not have a physical location, Instagram's geo-tagging feature can still have an unconventional use - as extra promotional space. When a geo-tagged photo is viewed either on the app or your web profile, the location given is listed right at the top of the content (just below your username but above the photo or video), and is the *first text associated with your content that a user sees*, particularly if the content's caption is hidden. As an example, the sports brand Puma, which does not have a single dedicated physical location, geo-tags its photos with a random location, but

172

gives that location a *name* associated with the product or message in their photo or video.

Use the Explore tab for inspiration

Use the Explore tab (the compass points icon) to see the latest emerging trends on Instagram, and consider implementing them in your own work. You never know, some of the tricks-of-the-trade that you pick up in this section of Instagram by searching with keywords and hashtags could help spark the inspiration that ends up producing your best piece of work.

Find and invite friends

Users like to follow other users who have a lot of followers, so getting off to a strong start is essential. Getting friends from other social networks to follow your Instagram account is crucial for building an initial follower base. Click the "Find friends" button in Instagram settings to add friends from your Facebook, Twitter or address book; or simply search for usernames and names of people you know who may be using Instagram already.

Share your photos across social media

One of the best ways to draw more attention to your Instagram activity is to share your Instagram creations to other social media, including Facebook, Flickr and Tumblr. In Instagram's "Sharing Settings" menu (found under the "Preferences" label of your account options), enter your social media usernames and passwords for the various accounts on offer, to make sure your Instagram photos are seen by your various followers on each site when you publish them. Where Facebook is concerned, you can even choose to send posts direct to your Facebook business Page instead of your personal profile.

Promote your Instagram account offline

Telling all of your online followers about your Instagram account is all well and good, but don't forget to let your real-world customers and clients in on the game too. In essence, put your Instagram URL details wherever your customers are likely to come across them: on business cards, receipts, letterheads, on a notice at your cash register, on your car's bumper sticker, in your email signature, etc. The possibilities are vast!

Give a reason to follow you
Tempt new followers by giving them a reason to follow you - write it in your Instagram bio, highlighting some of the stuff we talked about in the *'How to use Instagram for business'* section in this chapter. Remind people that they'll be among the first to know about special offers and promotions, first to get a sneak peek at new product lines, and have the first chances to enter Instagram competitions to win stuff!

Link to online Instagram Gallery from your own site or blog
Got a website? Don't forget to add a link to your official online Instagram profile or webstagram (more on these in a later section) from there to announce your Instagram presence to your visitors, especially those browsing on mobiles. If you blog, using your Instagram photos in your blog posts (and linking to your Instagram profile) is another great way of marketing your business to potential followers. In November 2012, Instagram rolled out official Badges that you can embed on your websites to promote your Instagram activity. Sign into your Instagram web account and choose "Badges" from the left-hand menu. In addition to a set of pre-made badges, there is also the option to download and customize your own icon.

Leave meaningful comments
Commenting on other Instagrammers' work is a great way to pepper your username around the app, especially if you are

complimenting a customer who is featuring your brand or product. To increase the chances that other users will click through to check you out, leave meaningful feedback and interesting comments. Ask questions about how a certain photo was taken, compliment the composition, politely provide suggestions to improve a shot, etc. All of this is good karma and will eventually lead to more followers. Search Instagram for users who have mentioned your brand name or hashtags, and comment to let them know you appreciate it.

Don't neglect your existing followers
To help maintain and grow your follow base, don't forget to check in with the activity of your existing followers. Use your Instagram feed to 'Like' other photos, leave great comments and thank people who leave comments on your photos. A good rule of thumb for growing a following is to like and comment on two photos from other photographers for every occasion that one of yours is interacted with.

Track and analyze your Instagram activity
Statigram (http://statigr.am/) is a free analytics service that provides a variety of metrics for your Instagram account, including your Top 5 most-liked and followed photos; how often you use filters and which are your favorites; and your most engaged followers. Sign in with your Instagram details and use the stats to work out which photos are most popular, and use this as a basis for future shots. Don't forget, too, that you can use a service like bit.ly (http://www.bitly.com) to shorten links and track their visits. Links aren't clickable within Instagram photo captions, but they *are* in your Instagram Bio, which you can direct people to via a message underneath a photo or video that you post.

Embed your Instagram photos and videos

When you view an Instagram photo or video (more on these shortly) on your desktop web browser, you'll see a share button on the right-hand side (just under the comments button). Click this button and you'll get an embed code that you can copy and paste into your website, blog or article. Handily, the embedded image or features an Instagram logo, when clicked, will take viewers to your Instagram profile where they can discover more of your content.

Taking Great Instagram Photos

Don't take your photos in Instagram

To produce the best Instagram photos, this is probably the most important tip in the whole chapter. Instead of taking your photos from within the Instagram app, where your pre and post-shot options are limited, take the original photo with your phone's default camera. This will provide you with a 'clean' image that can be imported into more advanced photo editing apps - with more filter, lighting, and color options -, and then onto Instagram at your leisure for final tweaking and publishing - it's how the pros get such great photos, and ones that look so different to anything that Instagram alone can produce. Check out apps like VSCO Cam and Afterlight to get you started.

Save your original photos

If you do just want to solely use Instagram to take photos, it is good practice to save an original copy of your photos to your camera roll at the same time. This will allow you to tweak the full resolution original as much as you like in future, should you not be happy with the Instagram snap. From your Instagram profile in the app, click on the cog icon and make sure "Save Original Photos" is switched on.

Keep it simple

Some of the best pictures are the most simple - a single flower, a bug, a tree, a bird, especially where mobile photography is concerned; don't risk overcomplicating the frame with tons of different elements. That doesn't mean that you can't take great photos with lots of people or things in it, but where Instagram is concerned, they often appear as too busy or noisy.

See the world in squares

One of the most important things to remember about Instagram is that photos are uploaded as squares like an old Polaroid snap; landscape and portrait images will need to be cropped or scaled, or moved before they are published, or you will be left with big black borders. So even before the shutter closes on your widescreen camera view, try and imagine how your composition might appear as a square on Instagram.

See things differently - angle it up

Instagram encourages you to see the world in a new way. We're all so used to viewing the world from head height, so experiment with high and low perspectives, and from as many different angles that you can muster.

Tap to focus

One of the easiest mistakes to make (especially with the instant photo-taking experience on a mobile phone) is to place the focus on the wrong part of the composition. The iPhone and other phones do attempt to focus automatically, but only guess because it doesn't know *exactly* what you want to focus on. By tapping the screen to focus on your subject before you take the photo, the quality of your finished photo will be much clearer (i.e. less blurry!).

Auto exposure/auto focus lock

Despite tapping to focus, sometimes the focus or desired exposure can be lost when you move your phone around. To prevent this on iPhone, tap and hold on the area of the screen you want to focus on. When the blue focus box surges and blinks twice, you can release your finger; you should see the message "AE/AF Locked" at the bottom of the screen. If you try moving your camera around, this focus and exposure will remain constant. To remove the AE/AF Lock, just give another quick tap.

Headphone trick for perfect focus every time
Tapping your iPhone's screen to take your shot after you've got the perfect framing and focus can jolt you out of position and blur the image as it's taken. To prevent this, you can use your headphones as a cable release in order to take photos without having to touch the screen. Plug in your Apple headphones, and touch the 'volume up' button to take a photo while in the Camera app.

The rule of thirds
Just with other forms of photography, the 'rule of thirds' is deeply rooted in many of the great Instagram shots. Imagine your viewfinder is split into thirds, both horizontally and vertically (or turn on the iPhone Camera grid view via Options); now balance your composition between these areas. Remember that Instagram will force you to crop or scale your image into a perfect square, so bear this in mind before you upload.

Master the crop tool
A good picture can become a great picture when it is cropped correctly. Currently, you can't crop a photo you take within the app, but you *can* if you import it first. Cropping allows you to eliminate unwanted noise or create a cleaner composition, focusing fully on the most important element(s) of the shot.

Invest in a tripod

Of course, the fun of mobile photography comes in being able to snap to your heart's content at a moment's notice. However, for more carefully considered shots, you might want to invest in a tripod to keep your phone steady, or to position it steadily and securely at all kinds of interesting angles. Traditional cell phone tripods can be picked up for around $10, or you can plump for the much more versatile Gorillapod, a super portable tripod with bendy legs that can stand on or wrap itself around almost anything.

Straighten your photos

Without a tripod, it is all too easy to take Instagram photos that are crooked. Very rarely does this improve a photo, so always remember to straighten your work in post-production, using the tool provided on the screen displayed after you snap a photo in Instagram. Tap the icon that looks like a photo frame with a dotted line through it.

Turn on HDR

HDR (High Dynamic Range imaging) is a process that that takes multiple exposures of an image instead of just one (one over-exposed, one under-exposed, and one in the middle) and then combines them in order to bring out all of the details of that photograph, with a greater range of light and shadows and more detail. It works best with cityscapes and landscapes. Turn it on, using the options in the center of the screen when you load the iPhone camera app on an iPhone. Alternatively, grab an app to do the same thing. Try TrueHDR and Dynamic Light (both iOS), or Pro HDR Camera (Android).

Do you really need a filter?

The filters are there, so why not use them every time, right? Wrong... sometimes. That old adage 'less is more' applies to Instagram photos too. Carefully consider whether a filter really does improve the look and feel of the photo before sharing it. If you really can't bear to upload your snap untouched, you could play around with the blur, contrast or brightness in an app like Camera+ for a more subtle change.

Use Lux to fix underexposure
Instagram v2.1 introduced a feature called Lux, which transforms photos that are underexposed or lack contrast, with a simple tap. After you take a photo within Instagram, tap the sun-like icon in the lower bar to apply the effect. Lux is especially good for landscapes and cityscapes, where lighting may be poor and shadows dim your images. Combine Lux with a filter for added impact.

To flash or not to flash
Choosing whether or not to use flash can have a big impact on the outcome of your photos, so use it wisely. By default, most phones' flash is set to Auto, which works OK most of the time; but take control and go manual for the best results. When to use flash? In daylight when shadows shroud your subject, and in darkness. When NOT to use flash? Large arenas, concerts, sporting events, mirror photos or when shooting through glass.

Play around with colors
One great way to make regular photos really POP off the screen is to add selective color to certain elements. Imagine a photo of a rose flower, all in black and white but for the vibrancy of the red flower, for example. Apps such as Colorize and Colorizer (iOS) and Color Splurge (Android) are perfect for experimenting with these kinds of effects.

Use the tilt-shift option to make photos look like toy towns
One of the biggest emerging trends in photography in recent times is the tilt-shift lens. These add blur to certain sections of a photo, tricking the eye into seeing an image that turns real life into a

living, breathing toy town. You can fake this effect with apps such as TiltShiftGen and TiltShift (iOS) or Awesome Miniature (Android), or by using the in-built tilt-shift option in Instagram (raindrop-like icon in the top menu) to blur in a circle or straight line on your image.

Add light effects

To use light for impact in your photos where appropriate, consider apps such as Lenslight and Lensflare (iOS), or Lumie Light Effects (Android). These allow you to experiment with effects such as lens leak, bokeh circles, and lens flare.

Experiment with black and white and sepia

Converting your photos to monochrome or sepia can help accentuate the lighting and lines in a photo, often making it much more interesting than the original color image. If your camera app of choice gives you the ability to adjust your lighting, sometimes "overexposing" your picture can create some cool effects.

Get symmetrical

Symmetrical shots look great with Instagram. You'll finish with a perfect square crop of your image. When taking your photo, the key is to center yourself perfectly and make sure all your lines are dead straight.

Combine several photos

One of the most powerful methods you can use to bolster the impact of your Instagram photos is to combine several together in one collage, to give step-by-step instructions, tell a story, or give more interest to a particular scene or event. As mentioned earlier, apps such as PicFrame and Diptic allow you to do just that, with different layout, borders and sizes, until you are 100% pleased with the final result.

Overlay text

If you want to personalize your Instagram images with a call to action, question, inspirational quote, or other text, consider apps such as Phonto (iOS) or Pro Paint Camera (Android) to create the effect. Both feature a variety of fonts and colors, and the photo can then be imported straight into Instagram for touching up and sharing.

Double-tap to like strategy

As you scroll through the Instagram feed on your smartphone, you can quickly and easily 'like' a photo by double-tapping it; a white heart icon will pop up to let you know it worked. To unlike a photo, double-tap again. Encourage fans to use this method to easily 'like' your content. One year, Coca-Cola used the slogan "Double-tap to unwrap" alongside a packaged Christmas gift as a way to encourage fans to engage. When the photo hit a set amount of likes, Coca-Cola revealed the hidden present. You can use the same tactic as a method to "unlock" special offers or price discounts on your products or services.

Mention another user

There are two places you can tag (or @ mention) another Instagram user: in the caption before you publish a photo, and in a comment. To mention someone in a caption, just type @ followed by the username, e.g.@bobthebob. When you publish the photo, the username will be linked to the corresponding profile, and the user will be notified that they were tagged. If you want to reply to someone's comment on a photo, tap and hold the username and select "mention user."

Editing captions and deleting comments

There is currently no way to modify a caption once you have published a photo, but you can delete the whole photo by choosing the "Delete" option from the menu represented by three little dots below your published snap. As for deleting comments, go to the one you want to remove, then swipe right-to-left across it to make a Delete button appear.

Recording Video in Instagram

In June 2013, video recording was rolled out to Instagram. The feature allows users to film clips of up to 15 seconds long to share with the app's huge community and across other social media. The following are a selection of tips to help you make the most out of shooting video for Instagram.

Plan your shoot, record outside of Instagram

As editing on the fly is so limited within the Instagram video app, it is wise to plan in advance your recording, and the shots that you will use, if you are going to go down this route. If you have more time, however, do take advantage of functionality that was added to Instagram in August 2013 - specifically, it now allows users to import video clips from their phone's camera roll to be trimmed, tinkered with, and published to Instagram. Without being forced to record within Instagram, you are free to use your phone's own camera and/or other apps to create potentially more compelling content, before sharing it to a wider audience via your Instagram profile. Some good options include combining your phone's native camera with video editing and filter-adding apps like iMovie, Vintagio, and 8mm Vintage Camera (iOS) and Magisto or Videocam Illusion (Android).

Your video is how long?!

Although the maximum length of record time for a video clip on Instagram is 15 seconds, you do not have to use it all up in order to post a clip; in fact, the minimum length of a video is just 3 seconds. Considering the way that users engage with social media, 15 seconds is a *lifetime* to spend watching a video - especially if it is purely promotional. In respect of this, I would not advise that you make your Instagram videos 15 seconds long on a consistent basis. With Vine videos (Instagram's main competition, and discussed in the next section) lasting a maximum of only six seconds, this general time frame, in my opinion, is preferable.

Jerky camera work? Turn on "Cinema" mode

One of the features Instagram is most proud of is *Cinema*. With the tap of a finger, Cinema aims to remove as much wobble from your video as possible, making it seem as smooth and professional as if it was filmed by a Hollywood camera operator with a Steadicam. At the same step that you choose a filter for your video, you will notice an icon of a shaky camera. Simply tap this icon to turn Cinema mode on.

Choose a compelling cover frame

After you have recorded a video and added a filter, Instagram will ask you to add a cover frame. This will act as a thumbnail for your video in the feeds of your followers and in search results, so use the slider to choose the most compelling still shot available from those provided. The more appealing the image is, the better chance it will catch people's eyes enough to want to check it out!

For more tips about the types of video content that resonate with Instagram users, check out the Instagram tips earlier in this chapter, and Vine Tips and Snapchat Tips chapters of this book.

Instagram Direct: Private and Group Messaging

In December 2013, a new function – Instagram Direct – was rolled out to the app. Instagram Direct is a private and group messaging function that allows users to send photo or video messages to select people – either to a single individual or to groups of up to 15 people at a time. Whereas in the past, any content posted on

Instagram was sent to the feeds of everyone who followed you *and* was publicly viewable via your mobile or web profile, Instagram Direct messages do not appear publicly.

When you send a message directly (after you take a photo or shoot a video and are done editing, select "Followers" to share the content with everyone or "Direct" to selectively choose who it goes to), you'll be able to find out who's seen your photo or video, who's liked it and also watch the recipients commenting in real time via the "folder" icon that sits at the top of the Instagram home screen. Photos and videos that you receive directly from people you follow will appear immediately in your inbox, but if someone you're not following sends you a photo or video directly, it will be held in your requests list until you decide that you want to view it. If you choose to view it, further private messages from that user will no longer need approval.

Instagram Direct is primarily being aimed at casual users of Instagram to share messages privately between one another, but brands and businesses can also take advantage of this added functionality. Here are just a few ideas on how:

Conduct customer service

Previously, any customer service issues that arose via Instagram were often forced to be dealt with within the comments section underneath a photo or video. Now, public disputes can be ushered into the more private setting of Instagram Direct. This prevents your comments being clogged up by unsightly feedback and prevents your brand image from being damaged. To make the transition, reply to a complainant in the comments telling them that you will send/have sent a direct message to them to help solve their issue, and then go from there. Photos, videos, and text can be used as a way to help solve problems - choose whichever means of communication works best for you.

To further enhance your customer service via Instagram Direct, advertise in your bio that people can contact you privately, and actively monitor negative mentions of your brand via your notifications and Instagram search to leap on and deal with problems before they get the chance to stew and escalate.

Offer coupon codes / exclusive deals

While occasionally sending coupon codes out to all of your Instagram followers is a sound tactic in itself, messaging them to an exclusive group of followers can be even more effective. Tactics include:

- Send a direct message including a coupon code to new or milestone followers (e.g. 50th, 100th, 1000th).
- Send a coupon code out as an apology for a customer service issue.
- Send a coupon randomly to surprise and delight a follower; encourage the recipient to share it with their friends both on Instagram and elsewhere.

Note: Make sure that each coupon code you create is unique so that you can track its success easily, and also limit the quantity and set deadlines for their use to encourage their use, and discourage abuse.

Give ultra-exclusive sneak peeks

In a very savvy move - and one you can emulate - Kardashian Kollection offered 15 of its followers an exclusive behind the scenes photo from its latest fashion collection. To enter, Instagram followers were asked to screen grab the image which told them of the entry instructions and re-post it with the hashtag #KKDIRECT. The promotion received over 4,000 likes and 650 comments in under 24 hours... and the really clever part? By requesting followers to re-post the entry instructions, they put their fans to work in helping to drive more participants. After the promotion, screen grabs of the private messages being sent to the chosen 15 were posted publically for transparency.

Run contests

Private messaging on Instagram gives you the chance to run more types of competitions via the app, and promotions that can be held "ad-hoc" with smaller prizes. Example strategies include:

- Hold a contest where the first person to reply privately with the answer to a question, or post a certain photo, or tweet with a certain hashtag wins a prize, e.g. *"The first 10 people to send us a photo of themselves wearing a Shawn's Sweater while standing in a bucket will win a $10 gift voucher towards their next purchase!"* or *"The next 5 people to post a video eating at Bob's Burgers with the hashtag #lovebobs will get a very special Direct message from us..."*

- Hold a "friend referral" contest where the winner is the first person to get 5 friends to follow you and mention the username of their referrer in the direct message.

- Host a scavenger hunt, where a clue is sent out at a time to an exclusive set of followers, and the next one is only delivered once you receive the correct answer to the first. The winner is the user who reaches the end of the hunt - in the real world or virtually (finding clues hidden on your website, for example) first.

Vine Tips:
Marvelous Marketing With Micro-Video

Vine is a Twitter-owned micro-video app that launched at the beginning of 2013. It allows users to record short, six-second video clips that play in an endless loop. These creations can be shared across social media; their brevity and scope for creativity makes them a great marketing tool for business. Many of the Instagram and Snapchat tips in this book (both for images and video) also work well for Vine, but this chapter highlights a variety of Vine-specific strategies that you can employ.

Note: Don't forget to grab a custom Vine web URL, available once your account is older than 30 days and has more than two posts. Once you select an available URL you will be able to access your profile on the web by visiting http://vine.co/*yourchosenurl*. Selecting a custom URL will allow you to share your Vine profile more easily and makes it easier for others to find and watch the content you have created. To register a custom Vine URL, point your browser to https://vine.co/profiles, then log in with your Vine username and password or sign in with your Twitter account. You can choose your custom URL via the Settings menu, but make sure you get it right as you won't be able to change it again after it is set.

On the mobile app, meanwhile, you can customize your profile with one of a number of colors. Simply visit the app's Settings to view and choose the color that suits your brand the best.

Technical considerations to make Vine videos shine

Think before you press record, save and edit sessions

Unlike snapping a photo or taking a quick video recording on the fly as you might do for a post to Facebook or Twitter, Vine videos work best when they are each planned and crafted as a mini project in their own right. With this in mind, it is important that you think about what video you want to make before you begin. Without wanting to make anything too complicated, it might even be useful to sketch out or list a quick storyboard of shots in advance. Plan what you will film, the angle and composition of the shots, and how long you want each shot to appear for, in order to produce the best end result.

Up until October 2013, recording with Vine used to be a one-take process: press and hold to record a clip, let go to stop, then repeat as many times as required - but the introduction of two new functions have changed all of that for the better. The Sessions mode allows you to save any recording and come back to it later, *and* you can work on up to ten posts at once. To save a new session or open an existing one, tap the icon that looks like a sheet of paper in the bottom-right corner of the app. Time Travel, meanwhile, allows you to remove, reorganize or replace any shot within a recording session before you share it. Tap the green bar from the camera while you're shooting, or tap 'Edit' when you're previewing a post.

Consider lighting and stillness

It might sound obvious, but Vine videos work best with proper lighting and a series of steady shots. This is even more important if you are a brand that is creating Vine videos to show off your products or services. These few extra moments of consideration - looking for a suitable place to shoot your videos, and even investing in a tripod to help keep your mobile-captured shots steady - could make all the difference to how successfully your Vine videos are eventually received.

Improving sound recording strategies

While you may not want to include sound in some of your Vine videos, the app will always record audio when it is being used. There are several ways that you can improve the quality of the audio in your Vine videos - from using a pair of ordinary headphones with a built-in microphone for better recording of your own voice, to an add-on directional microphone to better record the voices of others. For near-silent videos (other than telling everyone in the vicinity to pipe down!), placing your phone in a heavy duty weatherproof case often does the job.

Train your tapping finger!

As you know, every tap or press of the screen in Vine tells the app to record. With practice, you can easily squeeze 140 taps into one Vine, thus producing a video that is almost 24 frames per second. To make your tapping as efficient as possible, there are a few things you can do:

- Have dry, clean hands. Moisture on your tapping digit will cause the phone's screen to register a longer tap.
- Add a protective screen cover. They seem to allow for the smallest recording taps.
- Tap delicately! Hard taps may cause your phone to shake, which can ruin your video!

How to prevent auto focus in the middle of videos

The auto-focus function of mobile devices is unpredictable at the best of times; it can often cause an unwanted pulsation in the middle of a Vine video as the device attempts to re-focus on a subject. To prevent this from happening, set your phone down on a flat surface, use a tripod or hold your phone very still by bracing your arms against your chest as you record. However, if your subjects are moving a lot, none of these techniques may work.

Making unique Vines to help them gain attention

Tell a story

Vine's stop-start recording style gives you, as a creator, a lot of scope for experimenting with different types of shots and filming styles; don't be afraid to experiment. Although you only have six seconds, this is still ample time to introduce a beginning, middle and end to your clip; build tension and atmosphere; show subjects from multiple perspectives, and lots more.

Make a stop-motion animation

The standard frame rate for most smartphone cameras is approximately 30 frames per second, which gives you plenty of scope to construct some pretty awesome stop-motion animations on Vine within its six-second video length limit. This type of video can be extremely powerful and has been adored by people since the dawn of cinema, through to the advent of children's television and beyond to the current day. Vine's Ghost mode makes perfecting each frame of your stop-motion animation much easier, too. Simply tap the little ghost icon in the bottom-right corner of the app to see your last scene, which will be lightly overlaid on your current view.

Make an infinite loop

All videos in Vine loop infinitely when played, so use this to your advantage to create a video that rolls seamlessly. Instead of a video that ends abruptly (e.g. a cat jumping off a table onto the floor), try to find a way to smoothly transition the end of your video so that it naturally flows back to the beginning of the looped video. What you'll end up with is a mesmerizing six-second advert for your brand that viewers will want to watch over and over again.

Make a sound-only video

This tactic can be very effective, as it builds anticipation and forces your audience to engage with your video and use their imaginations to figure out what is happening. For example, you could have a black or white background with nothing but the sound of footsteps approaching, the sound of a marching band or the ticking of a clock - whatever you wish, really - followed by a mention or image popping up of your brand and tagline.

Make a 360-degree video

One of the coolest-looking types of Vine videos is a 360-degree swoop around a subject; it works great for showing off products, buildings and almost any other inanimate object. To pull it off, place a small piece of sticky tape to your phone's screen and mark it with a black dot. When recording, use this black dot as a reference point to make one short recording, move to the next position, and record again, as a way of making your circular path line up nice and level. To add an extra layer of smoothness and stability to the production, strap your camera to something like a glass tumbler or a toy car to act as a makeshift camera dolly.

Experiment with video length

Vine's maximum video length is six seconds, but you don't *have* to use up all of that time; often you will not want to. After about two seconds, a little check box will appear on the screen of the app. Tap this to stop the recording whenever you are ready.

Use panning to add drama to your videos

Panning is a technique that is often used to add drama to a scene, and you can easily replicate it using Vine. Walking slowly alongside your subject works fine, but if you want a really smooth shot, consider placing your phone on top of a toy with wheels, or a table dolly.

Make transitions and an open/close shutter effect

To add transitions between scenes in your Vine videos, hold and record a dark piece of paper or card over your lens to create a black screen between shots. Similarly, to create a cool "reveal" effect (as if opening or closing a camera shutter) hold a piece of paper over your mobile's lens, start recording, and then remove it quickly so that the light floods into the lens - it kind of looks like a Polaroid developing!

Feature relevant hashtags in your Vine video captions
Like Twitter and Facebook, Vine makes use of #hashtags to allow users to group similar types content together, and could get your videos found more easily in search results. The Twitter chapter of this book has much more detailed information about the best use of hashtags but, in general: when adding hashtags to the caption of your video (in addition to a description featuring a couple of keywords you want to target) keep them relevant, keep them short, and don't go overboard with the amount that you use.

Create an enticing "cover photo" for sharing Vines to Twitter
In October 2013, Twitter updated the way that Vine videos shared to the site appear in its news feed. Where previously a user had to click a plain link to reveal the Vine video, now a portion of the video appears directly *within* the news feed, giving users a taste of what to expect when they spot it. The preview that appears shows the *top half of the first frame of the Vine video you share*. With this knowledge, you can plan ahead and use the first-recorded frame of your clip to create a "cover photo" that will represent your content when it is shared on to Twitter. This can be as simple as a video title or a dramatic thumbnail that entices viewers to click - take a look at how custom thumbnails are chosen for effect in the YouTube Tips chapter of this book and follow suit. When you shoot your "cover photo," just make sure the detail you want to show is within the top half of the frame so that it displays as you would like it to on Twitter.

Private Messaging on Vine

In April 2014, a private messaging function - Vine Messages (or VM) - was introduced to the Vine app. To create your own Vine message (VM), select the "Messages" option in the navigation menu, record a video and then send it to one or multiple contacts; every individual message will create a separate, private conversation between you and the recipient. Your messages inbox has two sections: Friends (contacts on the app) and Other (people outside your network). Over time, you'll need to keep an eye on both for messages from customers. Vine Messages can be used for a number of different business purposes, including to deal with customer service issues, to offer ultra exclusive discount codes to loyals fans, and to accept contest entries. For more detail on how best to carry out these strategies, mirror the strategies outlined in the Instagram Direct section of the previous chapter.

Snapchat Tips: Self-Destructing Social Media

Snapchat is the newest major player in social media marketing. The mobile app (launched in September 2011) is a photo and video-sharing service centred on one simple premise that is worlds apart from its rivals: all messages shared between friends via Snapchat will self-destruct, never to be seen again. In most cases, photo and video messages - Snaps - will disappear between one and ten seconds after being opened by a recipient (the time limit is specified by the sender), and if the Snap is not opened, it will automatically delete itself after 30 days. The only exceptions to this rule are a "one-time repeat per day" option for any single snap, and Snapchat Stories. Before sharing content with fellow contacts, Snapchat users have the option to add filters, and annotate photos and video with colorful text and markers.

As far as the wider social media sphere goes, Snapchat is still very much an unexplored avenue for marketers. However, when you consider that a Pew Research Center study released in November 2013 found that 9% of U.S. cell phone owners already use Snapchat - around 26 million people - and hundreds of millions of images are being shared via the app every day, it is definitely an option you should consider when planning out your own social media strategy.

While media shared via Snapchat only exists for a matter of seconds, if you switch your thinking to view the time limit as an *opportunity* rather than a limitation, there are plenty of ways that it can be used for effective marketing. Think about it this way: when a customer is notified of a Snapchat message from you, first they're excited about what mystery it holds and secondly they know that as soon as they open it, they need to pay close attention as it will soon disappear forever. By today's standards, 10 seconds of someone's *undivided attention* like this - especially on a medium as personal as mobile - is gold dust! Like all social media, the best Snapchat content is framed in a way that mirrors the style that the majority of its users take advantage of the platform. Where Snapchat is concerned, this involves humor, sharing secrets, having fun, holding small conversations, and capturing "shareworthy" moments. With that said, let's look at some ways that you can make the most of Snapchat for your business...

Ask simple questions questions

As the ability to type long text replies is limited by time and space on Snapchat, the best kind of questions to ask are those that are easy to digest and demand a visual response, either by photo or video. For example, a shoe brand might ask their fans something as simple as "Show us your shoes!" or "Snap us a photo when you're in store!". The quicker and easier you make it for fans to respond, the better.

Note: If you share a video snap, it often pays to add a caption that reads "Turn your sound on!". If the user's phone is on mute and they don't get the message quickly, they're going to miss what you have to say.

Have fun, be funny

Snapchat's majority audience is teenagers and young adults, and the app is dominated by fun and humorous pieces of content. If your brand image allows, don't be afraid to have a little fun - pull faces, doodle on top of your snaps, use Emoji emoticons to tell a story, or surprise your audience with something that might raise an eyebrow or two! If you can capture the imagination of fans in this way, the more likely they are to keep opening the snaps you send... which means the odd promotional one, too.

Show sneak previews

Snapchat media's brevity makes it a great platform for showing a sneaky peak behind the curtain of your business, whether it's news of a new product launch, an upcoming offer, or something else exclusive only to your friends on the app. If needs be, tease out the content over the course of several snaps to keep it digestible and to encourage people to look out for more. MTV UK used this marketing method several times to preview photo stills and video clips from the new season of its reality television show, *Geordie Shore*. The content was memorable and impactful, reminding people to watch the program and visit its website.

Offer coupons and special offers

Use Snapchat as a way to send out time-limited coupons or special offers to your customers. As the promotion will be seen so briefly, make sure that your message is extra clear and succinct, e.g. "10% off today only with promo code SNAP" *and* consider sending out a "heads-up" snap to alert people to the day and time that a promotion will be landing in their inbox. The 16 Handles ice-cream chain put an interesting spin on this strategy. First, they asked customers to send them a photo via Snapchat of them eating the chain's ice-cream. 16 Handles would then reply with a coupon code for money off their next purchase. The customer had to keep the self-destructing message unopened until they placed their order at the register, then quickly show the cashier the coupon to receive a discount.

Hold a Snapchat contest

As you know, contest can be a highly effective way to boost engagement and awareness of your brand on social media, and it is no different on Snapchat. Here are several methods you can use:

Scavenger hunt: Share photo or video clues to a secret destination, either in the real world or online, and allow your followers to compete to be the first to find it.

Word or picture quiz: Similarly, send out word or picture clues over a set period of time, building up to a way that followers can win a prize, e.g. visiting a special page on your site to enter a keyword revealed over the course of a week, or by sending back a specific snap.

First snap wins: Simple and sweet, this one. You send out a photo or video asking followers to snap back something specific or tweet you a screen grab from a snap, and the first one to do it wins a prize.

Take advantage of Snapchat Stories

The Snapchat Stories mode allows you to join multiple snaps together to create a rolling 24-hour reel of content for *all* of your followers to enjoy again and again. When any snap added to your story ages over 24 hours, it disappears and must be replaced with new photos or videos if you want the story to remain active. If no new content is added to your story, it will disappear once the newest piece of content expires, and a whole new story will need to be created. To add content to a story, just choose the 'star' icon after taking a photo or recording a video with the app.

While the previous Snapchat content strategies in this chapter allow you to specifically target individuals, stories are more of a "catch all" approach that give followers a better opportunity to view collections of snaps multiple times, and they also act as a central hub to which you can direct fans when you want them to engage with your Snapchat efforts over a prolonged period of time and enjoy a more substantial narrative of events. For example, the Washington Wizards basketball team uses stories to document its match days, making snaps that show the players arriving, a glimpse of the locker room, half-time fun, and the result at the end of the game. Similarly, the fashion brand Jack Wills employs stories to allow its fans to tag along all day at photo shoots for its newest ranges of clothes, while the online food-ordering service GrubHub uses stories to give its fans extra time to catch its latest promotion blasts and coupon codes.

How to upload content from outside of the Snapchat app

Snapchat does not yet include an official way to import photos or videos for sharing with your contacts; any content must be created on-the-fly within the app before being posted right there and then. For brands who want to pre-plan and pre-edit snaps before sharing them with the audience, this omission could be quite troublesome. However, the third party creation *LaterSnap* (available in the iOS App Store) offers a solution to this problem by allowing you to choose photos or videos saved in your Camera Roll for posting to Snapchat, and even comes with its own set of editing features to boot. As this is a third party app, not endorsed by Snapchat, do use it at your own risk.

How to grow your Snapchat following

Other than the obvious "market your Snapchat presence and username everywhere", one of the simplest ways to encourage the growth of your audience on Snapchat is to ask existing followers to encourage their friends to add you on the app. When asking existing fans to refer their friends, make sure you get them to snap you the name of the friend who will be adding you, and when they do, send both users a little reward as a thanks (discount code, unique content, etc.)

Combine Snapchat with other social channels

Given Snapchat's fluid and destructive form of messaging, it often helps to combine the app with other social networks as a way to switch up or more easily preserve the momentum of your strategy. For example, you could launch a contest using a Snapchat story, but ask fans to submit their entries to you via Instagram or Twitter, using an @mention and a specific hashtag. Not only would this help you tell how effective your Snapchat marketing is, but also provide some extra exposure on other social networks.

How to track customers on Snapchat and measure ROI
Unlike some of its rivals, Snapchat does not yet feature a dedicated set of tools for businesses to manage and track their activity on the app. Since this is a task most brands will want to carry out, some out-of-the-box thinking is needed until a time when official means of carrying it out is possible. Here's one strategy that I suggest:

- In a spreadsheet, list every user who adds you as a friend on Snapchat (use the Snapchatters Who Have Added Me menu to find them), and in the adjacent column, enter the date that they added you. Update this list once per day.

- After updating the list, send out a welcome message to the people who added you as a friend within the last 24 hours. Thank them for adding you as a friend and tell them to look out for an offer from you soon. In a new column on your spreadsheet called "Welcome Message," add a check mark next to the users who have received a welcome message.

- Within 48 hours of a new user adding you as a friend, send out one or more offer snaps to them depending on how much space you need. In it, feature a specific discount code, hashtag, or shortened URL that you can track visits to or mentions of, e.g. 10% off their first order with code X or free shipping if they tweet with the hashtag #X, etc. If you think your customers will be receptive to it, point them to a sign-up form for your newsletter, too. In a new column on your spreadsheet titled "Offer," place a check mark to all new fans who have received the offer snap.

- Schedule and send out more general pieces of content to all of the fans who have received welcome and offer snaps in order to keep them familiar and engaged with your brand on Snapchat. Mark these as sent next to the relevant usernames in your spreadsheet, then repeat from the beginning.

Note: If you're feeling brave, you can create multiple welcome and offer messages to A/B test which ones work the best, and continue to tweak them until your initial snaps are optimized.

I'll be the first to put my hands up and say that this is not the most efficient or eloquent of solutions for measuring the success of Snapchat marketing, but it's one of the simplest and effective available to us so far.

Foursquare Tips:
Check out Check-in Marketing

At the heart of geo-localized social media is Foursquare, a smartphone app that gives businesses (particularly those with a bricks-and-mortar presence) a way to build strong relationships with customers by rewarding loyalty with special offers and other accolades. While its popularity has been affected by Facebook check-ins, it remains a viable option for many brands.

Claim or add your business
It sounds obvious, but get your business on Foursquare as soon as you can. It might already be there (set up by a user, because anyone can list a venue), in which case, claim your business on Foursquare, and do it now. It's important for analytics and monitoring your Foursquare campaigns.

How to claim a business
1. Create a personal account at http://foursquare.com/signup or log in.
2. Search for your business at http://foursquare.com/search then click the name of your business to go to your listing.
3. Click the "Claim here" link after "Do you manage this location?" at the bottom of the right sidebar (you may need to scroll down).

How to add a business
1. Create a personal account at foursquare.com/signup or log in.
2. Go to http://foursquare.com/add_venue and follow the instructions to add your location to the Foursquare database.

Create a Foursquare page

A Foursquare brand page serves as the go-to destination for fans who want the inside scoop from you on where to go and what to do. Once you create a brand page, you can engage your fans by sharing content such as tips at venues, brand check-ins, and offering them special promotions and experiences. Any content you post on the page is pushed to your fans' smartphones as they explore the world around them. It's also published on your brand page for anyone to view online.

There are two main requirements to creating your Foursquare Page:
1. You must have a Foursquare user account and agree to the terms (which you should now have done).
2. You must have a Twitter account. This will customize your page URL based on your Twitter username, and will allow you to reach your Twitter audience via Foursquare.

When you're ready to begin, visit https://foursquare.com/create_page and follow the instructions.

Upload a Foursquare page banner
As with Facebook and Twitter cover and header images, Foursquare asks you to upload a banner image to represent your business on its page. The image must be 860x130 pixels, be a GIF, JPG or PNG and a file size under 250kb.

Change your profile photo
Foursquare will link your page with your Twitter account upon setup and automatically borrow your Twitter profile image too. If you want to change this for your brand logo or other image at any time, click 'Edit' at the top of your Foursquare page, hover over your existing profile image and click 'Change?'. Select your new image and click 'Save'. Note: your new profile image will not show until you have saved.

Add a page description, and remember SEO

Enter a description to tell users about your business, and why they should follow you. You have up to 1,000 characters to play with here, but a couple of keyword-rich sentences should do. The first few lines of your Foursquare page's description will appear in Google search results for it, so make sure you fit in your most relevant keyword phrases here.

Add your Twitter account, website URL and contact email

The last few sections of the Foursquare page setup has space for your Twitter account details, your website address and a contact email. The Twitter and website link will be clickable in icons at the top of your profile page, so definitely make sure they are filled in correctly.

One added benefit to connecting your Twitter account to Foursquare is an ability to engage with your customers much more deeply. From February 2013, business managers have the option to display their Twitter handle when someone tweets a check-in at their store. So, instead of a tweet from a customer reading "I'm at Joe' s Ice-Cream Parlor", it will read "I'm at @JoesIceCream" (with your Twitter handle linked and clickable). It's a small change to help businesses encourage more people to check them out - and hopefully go on to check in!

Link your Foursquare account to your Facebook page

Foursquare will connect to your Twitter account by default, but you can also, if you wish, link your Foursquare account to a Facebook page to share check-ins and tips to all your Facebook fans. To do this, click Edit at the top of your profile and choose the 'Add Facebook' option.

Add page managers

If you are not the only person who will be making updates to your Foursquare page, you can specify additional managers from the 'Managers' menu on your page. To add a new manager, you can search for a person by their email address, phone number, twitter handle, or Foursquare user id.

Share updates on Foursquare

People who have checked in or looked at your business page will see your updates on their phone, which you can use to help entice them through your door – there's no need for customers to subscribe to view them. Updates can be anything, such as news about an upcoming event or a special offer you're promoting. You can create updates anytime, or re-use existing content or signage, to reach people nearby. Show off new menus, special deals and discounts, or anything you think your customers will like.

With Local Updates, you can also choose to share them only with specific locations or all of the locations of your company, to make them as relevant and hyper-local as possible.

Update from the Foursquare for Business app

At the end of January 2013, Foursquare launched a brand new standalone app for business users called Foursquare for Business, available for iPhone and Android. This app makes it easier for business owners to manage their Foursquare presence on the go, rather than relying on the mobile web or having a desktop computer nearby. With the Foursquare for Business app, managers can create a Foursquare update and easily cross-post it to Facebook and Twitter, see recent check-ins, turn specials on and off, and browse business data.

Use images in updates

Images allow you to engage and entertain followers in a much more powerful way than just text, so be sure to get snapping and sharing as part of your updates.

Add events to Foursquare listings

Since December 2012, Foursquare has allowed you to add events to the Foursquare listings they manage. Previously, event listing were limited to movies, concerts and sports, but now can be used to list anything, such as a fundraising event, a guest appearance at your store, seminars, group meetings, etc. to help you promote upcoming events. These events will be visible to users of the app when they're trying to decide where to go, when they check in at a business and when they view their check-in history.

To add events to your business listings, log in to your page manager account at Foursquare.com, and click the 'Tools' tab.

Pull customers from local competitors

When a Foursquare user checks into a venue nearby, and if you have a Special Promotion running, the app will let them know - and hopefully draw them to you at a later date. Knowing this, consider running Special Promotions often, especially tailored to new customers who you can draw away from your rivals and convert into regulars at your place instead.

Make your specials accessible and unique

The word 'free' is a consumer's most favorite of all, so encourage Foursquare users to visit you with a reward for checking in - a free cup of coffee, a $5 discount, etc. Don't offer something that is going to hit your profits, but do make it something worth visiting for.

If you're going to offer Foursquare users a Special, make it unique to them - i.e. not the same offer you are giving to non-Foursquare users on a daily basis. There's no incentive to visit and check in if everyone who descends on your venue is getting the same deal.

The small print
Remember to utilize the fine print when you're filling out your special - it could make or break your offer.

Set a fair end date to specials
Remember to set an end date for any promotion you run, especially if it's a limited-time offer or a one-day special. The last thing you want is to upset customers who are confused about when an offer ends, or to let an offer you intended to be for a limited time get out of control!

Educate your staff about Foursquare specials
Be sure that all of your staff are aware of Foursquare and any special promotions that you are running. It'll reflect badly on you if a customer turns up flashing their smartphone, only to be met by staff with confused faces!

Your staff can easily tell when a person has 'unlocked' a Foursquare special (and can redeem it) as the color of the special on the app changes from grey to bright orange. If your register requires a code for discounts, add that code into the special. For instance, it might say: "tell the cashier that the discount code is '4sqDiscount15'".

Tell your customers you're on Foursquare
Start telling your customers about the fact that you are using Foursquare, and encourage them to check in. This can be done via all of your other social network sites, and is especially good on a sign placed prominently in your premises, such as in your window or at the point of sale. Include a call to action such as "Free coffee when you check in with us on Foursquare and spend $X - do it

now!" to encourage participation. Also, don't forget to spread the word about Foursquare on other social media sites, and add a Follow button to your website or blog. Grab them here: https://foursquare.com/about/logos

Encourage customer tips and leave your own

Foursquare lets users leave 'tips' to other users about why they should visit any given business, and they will appear on your Foursquare page. Encourage customers to leave their own (such as with a call to action on their receipt), but there's no harm in a little self-promotion either. Let your customers know what's great about your business, and leave helpful hints and cool info about your business on your own Foursquare profile.

Give timeless and useful tips

Foursquare tips can be timeless, or they can be submitted to mark a particular time of the year or one-off event (and deleted after it has passed). Be sure to take advantage of this. Tips can direct people to a certain place or instruct customers to try a certain item - you have the best expertise on your business, so use them to your advantage. Try not to leave Foursquare tips that are completely obvious - intrigue customers or give the kind of insight that will draw people in.

Check-in every day

Check-in to your own business every day (and get your employees to do the same). This keeps it fresh in the mind of all of your friends on your social networks. Include a comment along with the check-in, advertising that day's reasons to visit: new products/services, the start of a sale, extended opening hours, etc.

Use Foursquare as a loyalty card

As well as a bonus for new customers, consider using Foursquare as a loyalty card by rewarding customers for X number of check-ins. For example, a coffee shop might offer a free muffin for a customer who checks in and buys a coffee five times.

Promote slow business days
If your business is particularly slow on any given day of the week, use Foursquare to help increase footfall. For example, offer $X off for customers who turn up and check in on that quiet day or at a certain time.

Reward group check-ins
As an incentive for bringing friends to your business, an offer such as "Free X (drinks/appetizer) if customers check in as a group of more than three people.

Reward Mayors
A Mayor is the person who checks into your business the most using Foursquare. Reward them periodically for their loyalty, e.g. the Mayor at the end of every three months gets a free meal. Ask your Mayor if they wouldn't mind being featured in your store - why not include a framed photo of them for all customers to see, and to encourage them to want to become your new Mayor in the future.

Note recent check-ins to target customers
Following an update to the app in January 2013, a business on Foursquare can see more of their recent customers. Prior to this, businesses could only see the customers who have checked in within three hours. However, not everyone has time to check and note their most loyal customers several times a day. With a greater window of opportunity, make note of your most loyal checked-in customers' activity and use this information to better target future offers and marketing opportunities.

Create a partner badge

Consider creating a partner badge - Foursquare is selective about applications, but approval will help increase your followers vastly.

No physical presence?
Don't worry if you don't have a bricks-and-mortar outlet when using Foursquare, you can still make an impact with Pages and Partner Badges to reach customers.

Track your progress
Foursquare provides business page owners free analytics to help you learn more about the customers coming through your door. Here are some ways you can use the tool:

Measure your success. See how many check-ins you're getting each week, and how many of those are being shared on Facebook and Twitter.

Meet your best customers. Find out who the Mayor of your business is (the person who visits the most!), and learn more about your other top visitors.

Follow your activity. Each week, Foursquare will send you an email that includes key stats, along with any recent tips and photos that people have left at your business.

Blogging Tips:
Captivate With the Written Word

While blogging is the old man of the social media landscape, it still has *tons* to offer. Think of your blog as central to the social media content that you share elsewhere, and you will reap the benefits. A company blog is also a fantastic way to promote your business and engage with your customers. This chapter will reveal some of the best types of content to create in order to captivate your audience, and how to get your blog posts seen across the web.

Produce top content

This one should go without saying, but it is all-important in the world of blogging. Produce inspiring and educational content that is *shareable*. Make it really good and you can use this as the foundation of your social media marketing. Only post unique content; don't be tempted to pilfer and steal from around the web; it is very bad practice. That said, there's nothing wrong with being inspired by what others have written - especially if you think you can do a better job! Check out what others in your field are writing about, to help kick-start your thought processes.

Write effective headlines

Learn to write keyword-rich headlines that will make people want to read the rest of your article, especially if they see it in search results. Ideas include asking questions like, *"How do I craft amazing blog post headlines?"* or making references that tie your content into readers' interests or scenarios they often encounter, e.g. *"This is how America's #1 Mom Potty Trained Her Kids in 24 Hours."* Think about which keywords your customers will be using to find the content that you provide; replicate them in your blog post titles. For example, a customer is much more likely to search for *"how to bake chocolate cake recipe"* rather than *"Omnomnom, check out our great chocolate cake recipe"*. So your heading might read, *"Recipe: How to Bake A Delicious Chocolate Cake."* Your blog post's title is also the first, and perhaps only, impression you make on a prospective reader - so make it count.

Post regularly

Don't write one blog post and abandon everything - write regularly and visitors will visit regularly to see what is new. There is nothing more off-putting to visitors of your blog than to see that it was last updated in May 2007 and you haven't bothered to update since; it'll only reflect badly on your brand, promoting it as stuffy and stagnant, instead of progressive and dynamic.

Use descriptive URLs for SEO

For improved SEO, ensure every blog post URL is descriptive rather than just functional, e.g. www.yoursite.com/10-top-blogging-tips-for-business.htm instead of www.yoursite.com/post345.htm. On most blogging platforms, the URL is normally generated from the words used in the blog post's title. If you are able to edit the URL to make it even more optimized for SEO, and you think it can be improved over what has been automatically generated, go ahead and do it.

Spin hot topics into multiple posts

One of the biggest challenges that many bloggers face is creating fresh content, week in, week out. One of the techniques you can use to combat this is called "spinning". In a nutshell, it involves taking one important topic that you know your audience will lap up, and writing about it from a variety of different standpoints. Let's take an article about painting a garden fence, for example. Several different blog posts about that one topic might be: *'A Beginner's Guide to Painting A Garden Fence'*; *'5 of the Biggest Garden Fence Painting Mistakes'*; *'Video: How to Paint A Garden Fence in 5 Easy*

Steps'; 'How [Brand X] is Revolutionizing Garden Fence Painting'. Get the idea?

Create *versus* posts

The power of the Internet has given consumers more choice than ever when it comes to buying products and services, so much so that the decision is often overwhelming. A great way to solve this dilemma, and put together a great blog post, is the X vs. Y article. For example, a company that specializes in beds and mattresses might write a blog post explaining the pros and cons of sprung mattresses as opposed to memory foam. These types of posts help consumers make a sound buying decision, make you stand out as a trustworthy authority figure - and are easy to put together.

Create 'What is the best...?' posts

Whenever a customer thinks about buying a product or service, they want the very best for their money. You've probably thought and searched the same *"What is the best type of x?"* or *"What is the best way to x?"* These types of searches are extremely popular, so work on integrating them into your blogging content. Furthermore, it's these types of articles that will build your reputation as an expert in your field.

Create problem-solving posts

One of the main reasons that people search the Internet is to find solutions to their problems, whether it be how to sew a button back on to their shirt, how to house train their dog, or how a guy makes himself irresistible to the opposite sex. Focusing on the solution to problems, especially for businesses, is a great way to come up with new ideas for blog posts and attract web traffic. Think about the problems that your customers want to solve - and then use your expertise to tell them how you (or your business) can help. To use dogs as an example, a pet store owner might blog about the best way to stop your dog from barking, or how to teach it to sit or fetch. Think about how you can become an invaluable blogging resource for your customers *ana* for those searching for solutions to their problems on the Internet.

Break news

Writing blog posts about breaking news within your industry sector is not only one of the best ways to come up with new and original content, but it also positions you as an authority figure in the eyes of readers. So, keep your eyes peeled for all of the latest news within your industry, and share it in a blog post with your readers. Ultimately, you will increase the chances of getting more business, as your peers and consumers will see you as a leader in your field.

Create 'list posts'

'List posts' are extremely popular, as they can be read quickly and are great for sharing, e.g. *50 Top Marketing Tips For Your Blog*. There are three common types of list post:

Brief list posts are long, bulleted snippets of information that users can use as a platform to search for more detailed information elsewhere (sometimes useful, but not always the best way to keep readers engaged on your site!)

Detailed posts include using different weights of heading (often referred to as H2 and H3 headings) and provide more complex, valuable information - like these tips.

Lastly, there are hybrid posts. These, as you might guess, are a mash up between brief and detailed posts.

Ask for opinions

Asking for readers' opinions is a great way to encourage interaction and engagement. Close your blog posts with a simple *"What do you guys think? Tell us in the comments"* type of phrase. You'll be surprised how much interaction this garners, especially if the question you ask is simple and quick to answer.

Run a blog series

Give readers a compelling reason to return to your blog, by running a cohesive series of blog posts, centered around a particular topic. Be sure to tell them to return for the next installment!

Be open about pricing

When consumers search on the Internet for products or services, one of the most common queries is, of course, about price. Even though it is uncommon for lots of businesses to address pricing upfront, it is the first thing that customers often question. Therefore, if you can figure out a way to address the subject of pricing in your blog posts, and be more open about it, not only will you gain respect from consumers who will appreciate your openness, but you are more likely to rank higher in searches which include questions about price than many of your competitors.

Use multiple authors

Most of the top blog sites employ multiple authors to produce content. While this might not always be possible for businesses (depending on their size), there are plenty of reasons to lift blogging from a solo activity. These include fresh voices (which can develop spin on different blog topics); the fact that different authors can help promote the work they write for you; and perhaps, most importantly - you don't have to do all of the work yourself!

Guest post

Offer to write guest posts on other influential blogger's blogs, and provide a link back to your own blog at the bottom of the post in return, as part of the agreement. This is particularly useful if you manage to post on a blog that is much more popular than yours! As well as guest posting on other blogs yourself, be open-minded about other experts posting on yours, to help build a strong network of friends within your industry.

Include a call to action

While this might not be appropriate for every blog post you write, consider adding a call to action on those posts that you want customers to respond to. Do you want customers to ring you, email, come back to view a new post soon, subscribe to your blog, etc? A call to action works extremely powerfully when you want a reader to act quickly - such as visiting your store to grab the bargains in your latest sale, or to prepare their garden before the winter sets in.

Don't be provocative

Unless your brand can withstand it, don't post content that is likely to produce an inflammatory response. Your blog acts as a huge reflection of your business online so, as is the case for all social media, remain friendly and provide top quality, shareable content. The last thing you'd want to do is offend readers - your potential customers. Social media is just as ideal (if not better) at spreading bad news as good.

Give something away for free

One of the best ways to market to blog readers is to offer them something for free, or a discount for happening across your post. Use email sign-up to capture them, and provide them with more information on a particular topic, such as 10% off their next purchase, etc.

The importance of images

Images, if used correctly within your post can really help to increase readership and views. There are several ways in which to decide what image(s) to use for your blog post. These include an image that complements your headline; one that illustrates a metaphor that is part of the blog post's main idea; or a pic that will make your reader smile. For those of your readers who process information more visually, the images you choose can help them retain information about your post (and blog as a whole) more easily. And of course, great images are just begging to be pinned to Pinterest, where your work will receive more exposure.

Image alternative text

Adding alternative text (alt-text) to images is not just important for search engine optimization (they can't see pictures), but also helps visually impaired visitors. Alternative text is what pops up when you hover your cursor over an image, and it can be edited in the image upload process on most blogging platforms, including WordPress and Blogger.

Integrate social sharing

Be sure to include widgets to allow users to share your content easily on Facebook, Tweet, +1, and add to Pinterest above or below your blog posts. Even the best bloggers in the world don't get found without a little help from their readers, so you need to empower people to *easily* share your blog post with their friends, fans and followers. Visit any popular blog and you'll see an array of social sharing options above or below each post. There are plenty of ways to install and customize the way your social sharing buttons display, but one of the easiest and most popular options is through AddThis (http://www.addthis.com), which can place the buttons on your page in just a few clicks.

Encourage email subscriptions

Many people still love to receive updates via email. The harsh truth is that most people will never return (or will forget to return) to your blog for a second visit - so be sure to include a "Subscribe via email" widget in a prominent place on your page. By gathering email addresses, you have a ready pool of willing contacts with whom you can share news and updates at any time in the future. Be sure to let them know what they are signing up for before they hit 'Submit', so that your emails are not considered spam.

The blog post length

There is always plenty of debate about the optimum length of a blog post, particularly when you are dealing with an audience who is short of time, who can easily look elsewhere, and are forever skimming quickly through content. I would suggest forgetting about the word count, at least to a degree. Instead, focus on creating interesting, well-formatted content that web and mobile readers will love, whether it takes 100 words or 1,000. Don't let worries about the length of your post dictate its overall quality.

Celebrate milestones

As traffic to your blog grows, celebrate this in specific blog posts, thanking readers for their continued support. Use these posts to highlight your most popular content so far, to encourage new readers to go back and revisit, increasing page views and time on your site.

Tag and categorize effectively

Categorizing and tagging your blog content effectively will ensure that it is found more easily by your audience, as well as allowing you to focus and define the kind of stuff you want to write about. For example, a social media blog might have categories including Social Media Marketing, Analytics and Video Tutorials, and tags below each post - clickable and searchable keywords that sub-divide the categories. Tags might include 'facebook marketing', 'twitter hashtags', and 'pinterest'

The 'deep linking' and 'linking to other sites' trick

Whenever you refer to a previous blog post while writing, be sure to add a hyperlink to it, so that readers can go back and check it out. On that note, you want readers to stay on your page as long as possible, so if you link outside of your website for any reason, be sure to set the link to open in a new window.

Respond to comments

Always allow readers to comment on your blog, and always respond to their comments. Even if they're negative, respond in a courteous and friendly way. Readers will appreciate the time you take to reply to them, and other readers will be encouraged to comment as a result. Make it easy for people to comment on your blog, by only requiring commenters to provide their name and email address.

Comment on other blogs

One of the best ways to promote your own blog is to comment on articles in other blogs within your niche. Many blogs allow you to add a URL when you post (normally making your name clickable in the comment when it is published) - a great opportunity to add a link back to your blog. On that note, try to be the first commenter on popular related blogs, so that your name and website is the first that other commenters see. Make your comment complimentary to the blog in question, or interesting or insightful, so that readers are more likely to take notice of it and tempted to click through to your content.

Add names, titles and bio

It is common for readers to want to contact and communicate with the author of a great blog post after they have finished reading it - and not just in the comments section. Be sure to include your name, title, and contact information at the bottom of each of your blog posts, so that customers can clearly and easily contact you.

Make your blog mobile-friendly

As ever-increasing numbers of people browse the web using smartphones and tablets, they are hugely significant in the way you design your blog's visual layout and write its content. Some of the biggest free blog providers (including Blogger and WordPress) will automatically display their blogs into a mobile-friendly format, so make sure yours does too. From a mobile user's view, there is nothing more off-putting than clicking onto a blog, only to have to keep zooming and scrolling to read the text.

Try to avoid writing in long and complex sentences, and avoid extremely long paragraphs at all costs. Web readers have a limited attention span and skim articles, but mobile users are likely to be even more distracted. If you are writing a long post, be sure to break it up into short paragraphs with individual headings in order to make it as digestible as possible.

Monitor progress with Google Analytics
Use Google Analytics to monitor the volume and quality of search terms which are driving visitors to your site. Use the information you find to tailor the direction of new content - expand on the most popular topics and tweak or ditch those that aren't working quite as well. Check your Analytics regularly to ensure you're always on the pulse with what your readers like and want.

Add RSS subscription
Provide a 'Subscribe via RSS' button in a prominent place on your page, so that people can have your posts pushed to them in their Google Reader or RSS feed after they are published.

Offer press packs and portfolio
Put together an online press pack and make it as easy as possible for media companies to access it via your blog.

General Strategy for
Super Social Media Marketing

Social media marketing is an ever-growing, ever-changing sector, but there are a number of core elements that will help you ensure a steady foundation to your social media ventures.

7 Easy Ways to Promote Your Social Profiles and Gain Followers

Add your social profiles to your email signature

Think about how many emails you send per day. Now imagine each email you send is a chance for someone new to find out about your social media profiles. Stick your social media URLs in your email signature along with a 'Like Us' call to action, and a reason why people should visit and 'like' your Page, e.g. *"Like us on Facebook for exclusive vouchers and discount codes!"*

Blog about your social profiles and give reasons why people should like or follow

If you have a company blog, why not create a post specifically to promote your social media presence? Give your readers five compelling reasons why they should 'Like' your fan pages in a blog post - e.g. exclusive offers, news to their feeds, sneak peeks at upcoming products. Don't beg them to like you; just give reasons why they'll benefit and watch the like box numbers trickle upwards.

Promote your social media profiles in your car, office and on business cards

Anywhere you can display your social media URLs is free advertising for you. Just think how many people would see a car bumper sticker with your Facebook address on, or a sign in the office or store window asking visitors to follow you on Twitter. In addition, combine offline and online by letting the people you meet in real life know about your social profiles, by getting their URLS printed on your business cards, letterheads, etc.

Ask different sets of followers to like your other profiles
If a person follows you on one social network, chances are good that they will want to follow you on another too. For example, give some compelling reasons to your Twitter followers as to why they should join your Facebook community, much as in the example for your blog post promotion mentioned above. A tweet might read, *"Great discussion about our newest garden tool range happening right now - get involved!* http://www.facebook.com/yourfacebookpage.*"*

In addition, don't be afraid to directly promote your social profiles once in a while. Unlike the approach above, here you simply point people to your page with a message along the lines of *"Enjoying our tweets? Why not join us on Facebook too? Click here:* http://www.facebook.com/yourfacebookpage*"*. Create and save three or four different variations of this message, so that you don't repeat the same tweet over and over.

Share your Facebook statuses on Twitter
Whenever you publish something on your Facebook fan page that you think would also be valuable to your Twitter followers, consider sharing with them a direct link to it. To do this, click on the time stamp of your Facebook status update (a grey link that will read, for example, *"16 hours ago"* depending on when you posted it, to open it on its own individual page. Copy the URL from this page and paste it to make up part of your tweet. Of course, customize the tweet to tell users what they're clicking over to see!

Create QR code links to a social profile

QR (Quick Response) codes are barcode-like square images that, once scanned with a smartphone camera, can link to any webpage you desire. They're quick to create and can be placed anywhere, either big or small, such as on print adverts, brochures or product packets. While QR codes are useful social media tools, don't put them in silly places... like your Facebook profile photo! Create customizable QR codes for free at a site such as http://www.qrstuff.com/

Ask your email list to like your social profiles

Got an email marketing list? Consider sending a dedicated email asking your subscribers to follow or like you on social networks - again with compelling reasons as to why they most definitely should. Whenever you send out future messages to them, include links to your social profiles underneath the main message.

More Tips for Social Media Success

Should I keep my social media posts short?

While many studies will advise you to keep text in your social media posts to a minimum in order to cater to low attention spans and mobile users, my advice is different. The reason? Studies like these will have covered a spectrum that includes text-heavy posts with low engagement that are often the result of poor writing practices, and short posts like memes that only generate lots of cheap, low quality engagement. My advice is to put the *quality* of your written content first and see how a mixture of lengths affects your engagement rates, rather than worrying about sticking strictly to a set character limit.

Use emoticons to increase engagement

Emoticons have long been used online as a way to express emotion with more lucidity than text alone can convey, and their significance rolls on into the social media era. A study by Amex

Open found that using emoticons in status updates increased comments by an average of 33%, while a separate investigation by Buddy Media discovered that posts with emoticons received on average 57% more likes, 33% more comments and 33% more shares. Not all emoticons are created equal, however. The same study by Buddy Media found reported that the best three performing smileys were :D (very happy), :P (poking out tongue) and :-D (very happy including nose). Posts that garnered the least amount of interaction included emoticons like :o) (happy with round nose), ;) (winking) and <3 (love heart). On the topic of emoticons, it's worth knowing that both Twitter and Snapchat support the use of Emojis - fully-drawn, expressive emoticons and ideograms that can add a whole new layer of fun and expression to your status updates; select them via the smileys option on your mobile device.

Don't post for 'empty' engagement

One of the biggest traps that lots of many businesses fall into is that of posting certain kinds of posts as bait to encourage likes and comments. The most obvious examples of this are *'Fill in the Blank'* and *'Click LIKE if you think X is X...''* sort of posts on Facebook. While these are great for occasional use, they do not give you a very accurate overview of fans and customers who are really engaged with your content, and how successful your efforts really are. Anybody can post an image of a cute kitten to get likes, but what real impact does it have on your fans' opinion of your brand?

Find a balance between influencers and brand advocates

Influencers are popular individuals or brands in social media whom you may approach to ask if they will promote your brand or service to their large following. Brand *advocates*, meanwhile, are highly satisfied customers. While offering a freebie to an influencer might result in a short-term boost for business, there is much more benefit in concentrating on building brand advocates. Here are some key differences between the two:

	Influencer	Advocate
Defined by	*Size of audience*	*Likelihood of recommending your brand*
Loyalty	*Short term*	*Long lasting*
Passion	*Questionable*	*Genuine*
Incentives	*Freebies*	*None needed*

Just because an influencer has a large audience doesn't mean that they will drive attention towards your brand, and they also have their own agenda for personal gain. Brand advocates, on the other hand, crave engagement from your brand, and are eager to support you on a long-term basis. And, of course, their trusted recommendations are much more likely to lead to sales. That's not to say investing in influencers is always a bad idea, but it is good to remember that the size of an audience should not be confused with the power to influence.

Appeal to the right people with contests

Contests in social media can work well in gaining fans and followers, but you need to be careful not to attract the wrong audience - i.e. those who just want to win something and aren't truly engaged with your brand. A smaller group of quality followers who may actually convert further on down the line are worth a lot more than a huge bunch who just want to enter a contest and win something for free. To help encourage the right kind of entrant, target the marketing of competitions to your audience via social networks, and try to avoid submitting to websites that exist solely to promote competitions; these are often home to the audience you want to miss out.

Search the web for social mentions of your brand
While I've touched on the different ways that you can use
individual social networks to discover and track mentions of your
brand, one popular (and free!) "catch all" solution to see real-time
activity, understand your content's reach, and get a top-down idea
of your brand reputation, is SocialMention
(http://www.socialmention.com)

Type in and search for your brand name and keywords related to
your company, and experiment with the different filters found in
the drop-down menu. For each mention found, the site provides a
set of overall metrics particular to it, including the sources it is
found at and whether people are interacting in a positive or
negative fashion. Hover over each metric with your cursor for a
short definition of each.

Free and Premium Social Media Video Tutorials: 200+ Videos and 8+ Hours of Content

Bite-sized YouTube video tutorials

To support the content within this book, I record and post regular social media videos onto YouTube. No filler, just free, clear and simple information that will help you with your social media marketing. The majority of the videos are screen recordings, with my voice guiding you step-by-step, and each major set of tutorials is grouped together into playlists for easy viewing. There are over 200 videos so far and that number is growing all the time, so why not head over to check them out? And don't forget to subscribe to the channel, so that you're the first to see future tutorials!

Subscribe to My YouTube Channel:
http://www.youtube.com/500socialmediatips

Comprehensive premium video courses

I also offer premium video courses on the website Udemy - an interactive hub for people who have something to teach and people who want to learn. These courses are considerably longer and more detailed offerings than my YouTube uploads; fully comprehensive guides to help you master different social networks and other related topics from start to finish. You get lifetime access to all updates once you enroll, and can even interact with me right there on the site with any questions you may have. Sign up to my newsletter and you'll receive a deep discount as a thanks, too - details on how to do this in the next chapter.

Enroll on my Udemy Courses:
https://www.udemy.com/u/andrewmacarthy

FREE Book Updates FOREVER

The very nature of social media means that the tips and tricks in this book will need to be updated and amended often. To prevent you from being provided with out-of-date information, *500 Social Media Marketing Tips* is updated regularly. To see a summary of all the changes made to the book over time, please visit: http://bit.ly/500smmtupdateslog

E-book version updates

An updated version of *500 Social Media Marketing Tips* is uploaded to the Amazon Kindle store at the beginning of every month, complete with all of the changes made in the four weeks prior. **These updates are available for free.** Unfortunately, Amazon's processes mean that you may not be notified when a new update has been made available, and in some cases it can take a number of weeks to hit your Kindle after I have requested that a new version be rolled out to you. I check for the update very often and let everyone know the good news via my e-mail list, so read below for details on how to join up and be notified.

The Kindle version of *500 Social Media Marketing Tips* is available at http://bit.ly/500kindle

Paperback version updates

Updating the paperback version of *500 Social Media Marketing Tips* is a little more challenging than its electronic cousin, so barring the requirement of a lot of important amendments, updates normally occur on **quarterly basis** - once for every season - spring, summer, fall, and winter. These updates will include all of the same tips from the electronic version of the book available at the time of printing. To check that you are buying the latest version, please look for indications of the version in the book's product description, on the front cover, and on the copyright page.

The paperback version of *500 Social Media Marketing Tips* is available at http://bit.ly/500paperback

Get notified of updates by e-mail

The best way to find out when new versions of *500 Social Media Marketing Tips* are available for both Kindle and paperback is by signing up to my e-mail list. I'll also share with you news about any of my new books, and links to the latest and greatest blog posts and video tutorials I create. *I hate spam as much as you do, so I promise that these updates will remain infrequent.*

FREE BONUS GIFT!

Sign up today and I will send you a free PDF copy of my report, *10 Essential Elements for Facebook Page Branding,* as well as discounts for my online courses and consultancy work.

To sign up, visit www.andrewmacarthy.com and enter your e-mail address into the box at the top of the page.

10 FREE Social Media Templates to Help You Build and Brand your Profiles

To help you design and brand your social media profiles in as awesome a fashion as possible, I have put together a selection of templates that are free for you to use. Each template is a .psd file that can be opened and used in Adobe Photoshop or GIMP (a free photo editing program).

The templates are as follows:

- Facebook cover photo template for desktops
- Facebook cover and profile photo template (optimized for desktops *and* mobiles)
- Twitter background image template
- Twitter header image template
- Twitter news feed image preview template
- Google+ cover photo template for desktops
- Google+ cover photo template for desktops and mobile
- Google+ profile photo template for square logos
- YouTube One Channel art template.
- LinkedIn Showcase Page cover photo template

For more information about each template and a link to download them, visit: http://bit.ly/freesocialmediatemplates.

Hire Me: Social Media Design, Analysis and Management

Since writing *500 Social Media Marketing Tips*, I have been contacted by many businesses who want help with their social media strategy - either from the beginning of their venture, or just for reassurance that they are on the right path. I am pleased to say that I offer a range of tailor-made, affordable one-off services and ongoing consultation packages to build and manage social media marketing for your business. My rates are very reasonable and negotiable dependent on your needs and budget. Services offered include:

- Social Media Strategy Audit / Analysis
- Social Media Profile Setup and Design
- Social Profile Management and Audience Building
- Social Media Strategy and Profile Design Analysis And Recommendations

If you would like more information on pricing or would like to get me on board to help you with social media in any way, please visit the 'Hire Me' page at my website, http://www.andrewmacarthy.com or email me on amacarthy85@gmail.com

I look forward to hearing from you!

About the Author

Andrew Macarthy is a blogger and social media consultant from Swansea in Wales, UK. His #1 Web Marketing Kindle Bestseller, *500 Social Media Marketing Tips*, helped thousands of businesses with simple, practical advice to optimize their social media activity and make the most of the sector's marketing opportunities.

In his spare time, Andrew enjoys running, Nintendo videogames, acoustic guitar, and Swansea City FC.

Any Feedback or Questions?
Email me at amacarthy85@gmail.com or contact me via my website or the following social networks:

Website / blog: http://www.andrewmacarthy.com
Facebook: http://www.facebook.com/500socialmediatips
Twitter: http://www.twitter.com/andrewmacarthy
Pinterest: http://www.pinterest.com/andrewmacarthy
YouTube: http://www.youtube.com/user/500socialmediatips

One Last Thing...

If you found this book helpful and believe it is worth sharing, please would you take a few seconds to let your friends know about it? If it turns out to make a difference in their lives, they'll be forever grateful to you, as will I.

In addition, if you have a few moments now to leave a short review on the Amazon product page, please, please do. Something that only takes you a few moments will help me out today and for years to come.

All the best, and thank you so much for reading *500 Social Media Marketing Tips*.

Andrew.

Made in the USA
Lexington, KY
18 April 2014